# WHY IS  N

## And Other Little Life Mysteries

### LAURA LYNN BONANO

## Foreword

*It has been a long time coming, but I made it, here's the thing I did. To everyone who made this possible, thank you. There aren't enough words in the world to vomit out that could express my level of gratitude. Still, thank you, for showing up, throwing down, and laughing at me.*

*If you're not a relative or friend of mine who is picking up this book for the first time, YELLUR! This is the part where I let you know that names have been changed to protect the guilty. I also make up words. I welcome you to the awkward phase of the party, where people start throwing away the cups to help the host, but something fun might still happen. I don't have the answers to the big questions in life, because I think looking at the smaller things is what makes it worth living, preferably without any pants on.*

# The Thanksgiving Incident of 2005

If I'm mostly honest, I never thought I'd do anything worth calling an incident, but if I did, it would have to be the Thanksgiving incident of 2005. It involved twenty rounds of card games with family, three pieces of pie, two bottles of wine, and my little brother's carpet.

I was living in between worlds. Home from college, I was old enough to drink, but not old enough to cut myself off at a respectable volume of alcoholic units. I remember every delectable glass of dark red from that first bottle of wine, the second one, not so much.

After a night of eating and drinking, mom eventually put me to bed when I could no longer hold my head up at the dining room table.

This shitface-edness was a far stretch from how I intended on behaving at home. See, I had the perfect example of how to ruin a life one beer at a time. Dad was my mentor in all things Heineken. At the height of my dad's drinking, I swore I would never touch the stuff.

Once I got to high school dad quit drinking, so living with a sober alcoholic for a father, there was never any booze in the house by that time. Don't mistake my soberness for smartness though. My early avoidance of alcohol didn't keep me from eventually sashaying into the world of cheap liquor and piss beer. I just postponed the adventure. Fortunately, when I did start drinking, I was able to procure Plan B all by my lonesome, not exactly in that order.

That Thanksgiving was officially the first time I was drunk in front of family, which marked my true exit from being a kid at my house.

Growing up, I had good reason to drink. Besides school, boys, and my thighs, as a tween and teenager, I had a bigger problem, I had a legitimate archenemy in the form of my little brother, Ricky. I always believed people were born with a purpose, and I was convinced he was born to be the literal Antichrist.

Ricky's legal name was Ricardo, but kids at school decided to call him Retardo (and by kids I mean me), so he eventually insisted we all call him Ricky. It took me a good 20 years to realize how awful of a child I was myself, as proven by my use of such a terrible word.

The level of hate between us went beyond, "Mom, he's touching me!" Our individual personalities put us at odds. My continuous singing of show tunes set him ablaze, and his sound effects while playing with action figures ignited my rage.

One afternoon, I was on the couch reading a V.C. Andrews novel for the sex scenes, and I became conscious of a sound buzzing in my bones. I was furious for no apparent reason, other than something was annoying me and I didn't know what it was. I had incestuous things to read about damn it, but some outer force distracted me.

In a flash, I jerked my head in the direction of Ricky's playroom across from the couch. There was no door to separate our disgust from each other. While a movie-siren-soundtrack of "REE, REE, REE, REE!" played in my head, my eyes zoomed straight to his mouth. I was officially on the warpath. Ricky had this way of using his lips to create a barrage of shushing sounds, followed by a "PEUSH, PEWUSH, PISH!" noise.

It wasn't just me who hated the sound. I can guarantee that every family member in the household had damaged vocal chords from pleading with Ricky to stop 'pishing' while crashing his toys into each other.

"Ricky, for the 666th time, quit making that sound!" I yelled at him, throwing my paperback down next to me.

He looked me dead in the face and calmly said, "No, I don't have to." He then continued playing with his toys and followed up with, "You know, you don't have any friends because you're fat."

My chest collapsed and I choked back a sob. It cut me deep, he transformed from being just annoying, to an expert in mental terrorism.

I pointed my finger at him and declared, "Oh yeah…well, if you don't stop playing with those dumbass Pokémon toys before you get to middle school you're going to get your ass beat on a daily basis…you little fuck!"

In a move I can only describe as supernatural, he grabbed a five-pound metal dump truck and threw it at my face.

I didn't exactly plan his demise, but I didn't actively try NOT to kill him at that point. He had it coming. I covered my nose with my hand and jolted up off the couch. My movements were not so supernatural, as my body was still going through that soft, squishy phase, where I was about as graceful as Donald Trump playing golf, white shorts wedgie and all.

"I'm getting the tuna fish!" I said, and I waddled towards the kitchen.

"No, no, please, no, I'm sorry!" he screamed as he chased after me.

Ricky was allergic to fish, to the point he had to carry an injection with him when we went out to eat. I'd often whisper to him that they probably cooked the french fries in the same oil they cooked the fish in, and he'd probably die and when he died, he would be in kiddy limbo because he'd never been baptized.

I yanked the tuna fish sandwich out of the fridge, but decided to drop it when he started crying too loud. I figured I couldn't have the neighbors know who did it when the police came sniffing around a dead kid next to chunks of tuna fish on the floor (P.S. the neighbors were my grandparents so that would have been doubly bad, they'd a ratted me out in a hot-fart minute). I managed to not murder him that day for purely selfish reasons.

My frustrations with living with Ricky weren't helped any from having to share a bedroom with him. *Side note*: We're in a non-judgmental zone here and you don't know my pain so just listen when I admit this next tidbit.

Occasionally at night, I would sneak up to his small bed on my knees and I'd hover over his tiny body, I'd take my thumb and forefinger, then plug his dumb nose by squeezing. I was just trying to stop him from snoring, not snuff his life out or anything. He usually gasped once, then breathed through his mouth, problem solved.

Parents, look, I'm not trying to tell you how to do your jobs, but if you have any choice in the matter, put your kids in separate rooms. This way, you'll know you've increased their survival rates with minimal effort.

I only almost killed him one other time. As we got older, we hated each other a little less and I'd give him rides to places in mom's Camry.

One cold winter day, I drove him to his driver's education class and I parked in front of the building to let him out. We mumbled our goodbyes, and then he got out to walk around the front of the car. Now, I'm not saying demons possessed me or anything, but I honestly don't know why I turned the wheel towards him and then stepped on the gas. It absolutely wasn't a conscious decision and I'm sure I meant to keep my foot on the break until he cleared my path. Before I realized what I'd done, he hurtled up onto the hood. It was a slow motion scene of him looking back at me with an utterly betrayed look on his face, along with terror.

The car screeched to a halt and Ricky slid back down, his feet hitting the pavement. I mouthed the words, "I'm sorry." He stood there for a minute, breathing hard, and then chuckled as he walked away. The pit in my stomach signaled how much I did love him after all. Who knew?

The day I left for college though, an even bigger shift occurred. Ricky stood out in the yard with me, next to a truck filled with all my collegy tapestries and three-drawer plastic bins. We stared at each other for a moment, and I initially had the urge to tell him I still hated him. Instead, I grabbed him to me and we hugged. He muffled something out that I can only assume was an "I love you," but could just as easily been "I loathe you." Just like that though, we weren't archenemies anymore.

Three years after leaving home that first time, the wine digressed me back into a bitter teenager. I didn't have any fights with Ricky since coming back for winter break, but apparently drunk me decided I had to establish my dominance once more with my little brother.

After I blacked out and mom put me to bed, I woke up the next morning slightly fuzzy and achy. Mom popped her head into my room with a smirk on her face. She shook her head at me and this was puzzling, because as far as I knew, the night was pleasant. Sure, I'd gotten drunk in front of my grandparents and probably took my pants off while still in the living room, but No harm no, no fly ball. Who hasn't done that?

"Guess what you did last night?" she asked. I crinkled my face up to make it look like I was trying hard to recall such allegations. Mom bulged her eyes at me and said, "You took a shit in the hallway."

I squinted some more. The statement made absolutely no sense. Who takes a shit in the hallway?

Miraculously, I had a flashback to the previous night. There was a flickering slideshow of me squatting next to the banister upstairs, holding on for balance. In my memory, my hair fell in front of my face, but I saw my pants around my ankles, my feet were planted hip width apart, and a draft swept across my cheeks. It all went hazy after that.

Lying in bed that morning I realized, Faaack, I had most definitely put a poop in the hallway. Mom's smile cracked even more as she said, "Not only did you shit in the hallway; but you stepped in it, after you stepped in it, you went into Ricky's room and like a dirty little ballerina, you slapped your poop-smeared foot on his carpet, just once. Then I guess you went to bed."

Sweating, I tore back the blanket covering me to see a brown smear on the heel of my left foot.

Mom admitted, "At first, I thought it was a dog poop, but then I realized, 'no that's a Laura poop'."

I shrieked and rushed to the bathroom to wash my foot off. I started to laugh uncontrollably. I would have been embarrassed, but I could only say to myself, "Ahaha, I got you, you little shit."

# Pecan Pie

In retrospect, I'm not sure if a tattoo parlor called "Wildman's," was the best choice when trying to foster peace, love, and harmony in my life. Nonetheless, I was home on break from college in Indiana, and it was time to begin healing for the first time in my life.

For me, coping with things never meant I let things out. I wasn't a big screamer or tantrum thrower. Instead I wanted to pack things in. My way to heal was by filling up the missing spaces with things that made me feel good, deliciously and painfully good. Sometimes it was through food, where I'd stay up late, sneaking around the kitchen, gorging myself on leftover cold fried chicken and olives. I would eat the food, but I never really tasted it. I was only thinking of what I was going to eat after the current meal. Even with a full belly, I'd meticulously plan out what I would have next because my brain told me I was still starving. The cycle could last up to six hours over the course of a night, consuming 3,000 calories more than I should have. The next day, I would swear to never do it again. I often looked in the mirror at my plumped face and place my hands over my double chin in a chokehold to hide the fat. Then, I'd ooh and ahh about how pretty I would be if I just didn't have that awful "fatness," I called it.

This isn't a story about an eating disorder though. My binge eating was just a symptom, not a diagnosis. I chose to overdose on a lot of other things besides food throughout life.

Another symptom in high school was my effort to fill myself up with other peoples' bodies. I tried to plaster my heart's holes with the love of someone else. Spoiler alert, their watered downed chemicals and pheromones never mixed right with mine.

I was never told anything about sex besides the fact that I wasn't supposed to do it. Surprisingly, the Indiana school system did teach me about the mechanics of fwapping genitals with others, so I was aware of how it was supposed to go down. The problem was, I never learned to date with my mind, and any sort of standards, so I banged a lot of guys way into college. This only provided forays in empty basements on bar stools and little in the way of learning how the clitoris was supposed to work. I don't think I have to tell you that the sex didn't heal me; it only created bigger holes...IN MY HEART! Shut up, don't you dare make a pun here, well ok, fine, make one because I set myself up here and it's your money, but it's my vagina so I still get to feel good about where it ended up.

Eventually though, I found something that worked better than anything else I tried to help me heal after various hiccups in life. I turned to tattoos (original I know). Now, I have ink imprinted into my layers, to hide the spaces I don't like. I decided that the weak, the soft, and the freckled surfaces of my skin weren't pretty enough for me. I couldn't change my face, and even when I changed my body through calorie restriction and exercise, it never felt permanent, like my body wasn't my own and the thinness would leave me as soon as I ate a slice of bread. I discovered that ink would stay with me. It was mine, forever. It wouldn't disappear after missing one run or fifty crunches.

The time in my life where I began to find my healing ritual was filled with a pain that I had become familiar with.

My freshman year of college, I was in the throws of an unhealthy relationship with Ahriman. Our "love," if that's what you want to call it lead me to eventually only changing my clothes every other week as my freshman year aged into sophomore year. In an effort to try something new to grow my confidence, I took up Aikido at school. I wanted it to be something I did on my own, but Ahriman insisted on taking it with me. I suspected he didn't want me making googly eyes at whomever I'd be sparring with so he had to keep an eye on me.

Forget what you've heard about Aikido and a certain celebrity associated with it and his love of the martial art along with his ever-weirdening appearance (name rhymes with Heeven Pagal). What I experienced in Aikido class wasn't the crazy fight scenes I had seen in the movies; the breaking of arms and throwing people over tables. Aikido was, and is more about self-preservation, a way to peacefully subdue whoever is throwing knife hands your way. The founder, a teeny tiny man shorter than my four-foot-ten inch frame, created it because he was tired of bigger peoples' shit and the fact that Brazilian Jujitsu didn't quite do it for him. I'm still waiting for someone to attack me to see if it actually works when I decide to use it. Aikido felt more like a dance instead of a martial art. I fell in love with it, while Ahriman struggled to replicate the moves and stances.

Maybe subconsciously I took the class because I wanted to protect myself from Ahriman, and didn't want to hurt him in the process by punching him square in the nards like I should have.

Ahriman was a fan of domestic violence. Often, after he hit me he would tell me I better not hit him back because his parents had put thousands of dollars worth of dental work into his mouth and I'd pay if I messed up his braces.

One day, I was glowing after class because I had been complimented and asked to join the Aikido club by the instructor, Guy. Ahriman saw my joyful face and decided for me, that I'd let him take my happiness away once again.

"You're not even good at it," he said. "The teacher only told you that, so you'd join that stupid club. They're desperate for members because they're all losers who roll around on the floor in dresses." I suspect he was just upset because he couldn't do a forward roll without looking like a toddler learning to stand up.

I shook my head at him and stayed silent. Then something started stirring. I chose not to believe Ahriman, and I became very involved with the club. I've never been very graceful when it came to physical things, but I was good at Aikido and I knew it. The instructor would stop class and call everyone's eyes upon me as I demonstrated a move. I even became President of the Aikido club.

When I came home on summer break from college, I was brimming with hope and a desire to change myself. Let's not forget the hours spent on long phone conversations, crying and pleading with Ahriman to believe me when I told him I loved him. Even a hundred miles away from him, he controlled so many aspects of my life, including whether I would sleep at night.

There was a saving grace though. More like a saving fireball of whiskey and a pure American Boy ready to show me the ropes of life again.

That summer, I reconnected with the on-again, off-again boy of high school, Jon. He was the first kid I knew who got a tattoo before he was even old enough to legally get one. He had flames and skulls lining his arms, but it couldn't hide the kindness in his being. He called me darling and despite the years of being unkind to him, he still loved me. I was officially an adult at 18 and spent the muggy hot summer season outside with him, hearing about his time in the military and his deployment to Iraq. His face had changed since high school and he had the thousand-yard stare. One night, we were talking and I traced the flames on his arm and decided I wanted to get a tattoo. The decision of what it would be had already been made. I wanted the word Aikido, which translates roughly to "The way of adapting the spirit." Hey, at least I didn't just pick a Japanese symbol off of the wall, only to have it mean, pineapple.

Jon said he would get me the first symbol of the word Ai, written in Japanese, as a tattoo for my birthday. He drove me to the shop and an artist made a stencil of the piece. The artist shaved a portion of my shoulder blade and quite abruptly dug into me with the tattoo gun. I'm sure my tattooist had a leather bandana on, and probably wasn't wearing a shirt, but this was still a legit, licensed establishment. The needles burned and ripped though my shoulder. Eventually, my skin numbed beneath the needles and I began to feel it down to my bone marrow. The piece came out clean and saturated a deep black. I spent the next week holding a hand mirror in front of another mirror so I could look at it. The symbol looked like a small hut with two walls and a simple thatched roof, swiped into form with soft brush strokes, instead of the actual stainless steel of the tattoo gun.

I would leave Jon that summer, to go back to my life at school, under the shadow of someone who had no idea of what it meant to be kind.

I don't remember when or how I got the remaining two symbols, Ki and Do, but they're there, I can see them. When I try to remember when I got them, it's like looking at a photo of a stranger who happens to be in a family photo. The younger version of you is there in the picture, on the beach somewhere and there are people around you living their own lives, never knowing you have a picture of them burned into your memory and plastered into your family albums. You see them, but you know nothing about them.

I eventually stopped doing Aikido when I graduated, but I still have the phrase on my body to remind me to always try to adapt. Most days I forget the tattoo is there, until I get a glimpse in the bathroom mirror, and I think of Jon.

I found my next tattoo online (again, I know, so original). It was a painting of a lotus. I was no longer with Ahriman, but his replacements had proven neither nice nor warm but, God did I try. I tried them all on like lipsticks, smearing them off when the shade just didn't look right on me, or they were too sticky, or too dry.

Craig was one of those replacements. He was the most beautiful boy I had ever seen. He rode around town on a BMX bike, didn't have a cell phone, and worked as a bouncer at one of the drinking dives in my college town. We cuddled on the couch one lazy afternoon, and when he saw a pregnant woman in a commercial for stretch mark cream, he admitted it was the sexiest thing he'd ever seen, and he rubbed my belly. It felt like it was going to last forever.

Mostly I just remember what it felt like to lie in bed with him. He was basically a gorgeous hobo, but a lot more hygienic.

The night I met Craig, my friends ditched me at a bar. There was dancing though, and I had no intention of missing out. I flailed around, gyrated and probably did some hopping about. Then this boy, this boy in my mind who I thought I had no business attracting, started dancing with me.

It was dark, but I could still see the colors of his hazel eyes. They were as if they had once been a bright color, but someone leaked the sharp brightness from them, leaving behind a pastel ghost of what they'd once been.

He was the first boy I truly wanted to be naked in front of, like there was no other way to be. He would slide his hand along my hips and stomach, and he followed it with a kiss and instantly I wasn't embarrassed of the curves I lived with for so long but had always hated.

Then I bought Craig a plaid shirt with my college loan money because that's what girls in infatuation do, they attempt to buy real love with gestures and desperate attempts at giving all they have.

One blissful morning after Craig had stayed the night, he told me we should go to breakfast at this diner he liked. He held my hand crossing a street, and I remember thinking, this is new. Ahriman once told me he was too embarrassed to be seen with me, so I had to walk behind him when we went anywhere together.

That morning, the misty air hung heavy. The streets were empty as we walked to the diner. I felt beautiful in my messy bun and sweatshirt. We sat in a corner booth with red cracked leather seats, the coffee was hot, and the smell of grease and stickiness filled the air. I don't remember how he looked, but more how I felt, talking and laughing, a distinct lack of fear I had been used to knowing with Ahriman. I thought it felt like a real date, not just a mission of getting food in our bellies.

Another quiet afternoon, we had nothing but time to learn everything there was to know about each other's bodies. After taking a shower, he lifted me onto the bathroom counter and proceeded to groom me with my razor. I don't think I had ever seen my own vagina, let alone let someone else glare into it with shear focus. Somehow, he made me not want to close my legs. I didn't care what I smelled like, or how I looked, for once in my life.

Six hours later, we had knocked a recliner over, moved the coffee table, and strewn clothes throughout the apartment, sore and achy, like after a long run.

We had been dozing on the couch, but eventually made our way to the bedroom for the real recovery, when I heard a knock on the apartment door. I opened it to see Cecylia standing outside my doorway, smiling and giddy. I had sent flowers that day to her work.

In my search for healing, I cared more about my own pleasure, than hurting someone else. I was not innocent. Cecylia was my girlfriend, and no one else knew about it, including Craig. Somehow, between midterm exams, hours at the Laundromat, and going to class, I managed to fit in dating two people at once.

The flowers I'd sent to Cecylia had been lavender tiger lilies, I think, though I'm not sure such a thing exists, but that's what my memory says they were. She rushed me and wrapped her arms around my shoulders, telling me how beautiful the bouquet was. I breathed in the smell of the black jacket she always wore.

I met Cecylia in the Aikido club. I had broken up with Ahriman and I quickly added her to my rotation, never asking myself if I was gay, only asking myself if she was too much older than me. We had become friends in the club and one night I drunkenly told her over the phone that I wanted to be with her. She was a geology researcher at the university and hesitant to let me into her life. Her black spikey hair was always styled as if she just didn't give a shit, and that made it beautiful. I told her I had been taking a nap.

"Let's put you back to bed," she whispered in her deep Polish accent.

"No, no, I think I just want to lie on the couch," I replied and turned around, trying to block her from the hallway to my bedroom. She kept walking forward, arms still around me. She told me it would be more comfortable in my bedroom. There was no way to save her from this. In a moment of absolute, forced honesty, I planted my feet and resigned myself to telling her the truth.

"Trust me, you don't want to go back there," I said. "There's someone else in my bed."

Her white skin turned even paler, and I'm sure I saw the exact moment her heart thumped an extra beat.

"I did love you though," she might have said, either that or some other heartbreaking phrase, I don't remember. She touched her hand to her crooked nose that I loved dearly, lowered her head and walked out. I went back in the bedroom to sleep next to a man who had no intention of being there the next day.

Through some random alignment of lives, Craig lived in the same apartment building as me. Well, when I say lived there, I mean his name wasn't on any lease and some kinder person than most let him pay her sporadically to have a place to stay. The only way I could contact him though, was to put notes on the door to the place he didn't actually live, asking him to come over. "I made dinner," the note usually said, and "would you like to come over, the door will be unlocked, it's cool if you can't, but I'll be waiting"…please, please don't reject me, I'd silently pray as I taped the notes up.

Eventually Craig stopped showing up at all. I tried on multiple occasions to reach him via more notes taped to his apartment door, when he finally sent me a message online.

*"Look, you're nice and fun, but, come on, it's pathetic, you always hounding me to come over."* Blah, blah, blah, insert more stuff about me wanting 'more' (whatever the fuck that is) and he just couldn't give me what I wanted. It was all just fine, but time to move on and leave him alone.

"But I bought you a motherfucking shirt with my college loan money, how do you even know what I want, you've never asked, mostly I just want to run my fingers along the little V's leading to your nether regions, and do you know how awesome I am, and how dare you talk about how hot pregnant women are without expecting me to imprint on you, you glorious bastard," I wrote back. No, that's a lie, I didn't say any of that. I just hemmed and hawed that he was right, and I said I was sorry I had bothered him.

Go back to a time he once told me he had slept with someone else and I rewarded him with a roll in the hay roughly five minutes later after the admission. Despite knowing he was not a good mate, I chased after him like a new mom chasing paisley print diaper bag at the annual Vera Bradley sale. I guess I'm to blame for that bout of heartache.

Give me a girl who grew up in the late 80's, started tweening out in the 90's, and I'll give you a woman who listens to Jewel after every Tinder date in the 2000's.

That night, after having the Hottie Hobo dump me, I dragged my mattress into the living room of my apartment, plopped down, and listened to a whole lot of the very popular, at the time, female folk singer on my Walkman. I swigged shitty beer and sang out loud for my neighbors to hear. To those that had to deal with my moans through the walls, I'm very sorry and I hope you're having a wonderful life now. Also, fuck you for blasting horrible music through the very same walls, I hate you.

I sang along to the sad songs through sobs and choking. The rejection didn't necessarily tear me apart, I was still whole, and always had been, I just didn't know it at the time.

That's the part that hurt so much. I was whole, but I still didn't make the cut. The idea that I took myself at that exact moment, and I was the best version I could be at that time; I was the hottest I'd ever been, the funniest, most adventurist, and cleverest I'd ever been. Then, another person took my whole, and said "no thanks." For years, I would feel like I wasn't enough. Are you beginning to see a trend here of me being just like thousands of women flailing out in the world...not being enough.

A couple hours after expending all my fluids and energy in grief, I passed out on the mattress in wet spots of slobber and saltwater tears.

Obviously, a week later I decided I needed another tattoo. I certainly wasn't going to drink myself into a stupor again, because of carbs. I researched a few shops around campus and settled on one. In the early morning on a Saturday, I had a neighbor drop me off in downtown Bloomington. I walked in the shop, nervous to be alone. I was told it would be a minute and my artist would be ready soon. To pass the time, I watched another client prepare for his first ever tattoo.

"Now, I'm going to draw about an inch-long line and see how you deal with it," said the female artist. She then started the buzz machine and touched it to the guy's back, doing a single stroke.

Thirty seconds in, the guy stood up and his artist pulled the tattoo gun back from his skin, telling him he needed to sit back down.

"Get me a bucket, get me a bucket," he yelled.

She put a trashcan under his head and the guy heaved and coughed up yellow, frothy bile. That, my friends, is why you don't get shitfaced the night before you get a tattoo.

"Just pick at the scab and hopefully that will pull out the ink, bud," the artist said. Then, puker walked out with his head hung. I sure hope he tried again one day.

I finally sat in the chair for my very own session with my handpicked artist, Chris. The other woman cleaned up her station, probably pissed about a lost Saturday morning commission. Thirteen hours, three cigarettes, endless conversation, and countless songs later, I had my back covered in a cherry blossom tree. My artist was kind enough to drive me home, and I was sober enough to not invite him in when he asked what my apartment looked like inside.

The next night, I was trying to figure out how to put vitamin D ointment on my entire back when I heard yelling and thumping in the hallway outside of my apartment. I poked my head out and saw Craig coming down the stairs, eyes red and watered down like a glass of ice and rum that sat too long.

Craig said something about his roommate kicking him out and another thing about a smashed car headlight. I said I needed help and he came inside. I handed him the tube of ointment and took my shirt off. He smoothed it on, inch by inch down my back. It was cold, then warm and I felt his eyes focused on me one last time. I thanked him and said that I was graduating in two days. He wished me luck and left.

I never saw him again.

This parade of madness repeated itself. I liked a boy, the boy tried me for about five minutes and said "No thanks," yet again. There were even more boys that I tried and decided "No thanks."

It wasn't that I wasn't enough at all. I think we all know that when we dig deep. I had always felt I wasn't tall enough, tan enough, bouncy enough, perky enough, small enough, smart enough, and quiet enough. I had to ask myself who and what I wasn't enough for. I decided it had nothing to do with another person's needs of me. I had to find what my needs were of me, and figure out how to close the gap on where I was falling short for myself.

I thought about it some more. Say there's someone who knows they don't like pecan pie, but they go out on a limb and try one piece. They don't look at the magical dessert and say, "Nah, wasn't enough pecan pie, if it had more pecans and more gelatinous sugar substance, I might like it, but probably not, because I hate pecans, and sweetness in general." Unless it's a shitty piece of pie from a gas station, then they're justified.

Meanwhile, pecan pie doesn't sit there on the counter and say, "I'm done, I can't do this anymore because people don't like me. I think I'll give up being a pie." That glorious slice of sticky glob, will never cry, shake its fist and say, "I quit." It won't do those things, because it's a seasonal pastry.

But, let's play pretend for a minute and imagine pie is in fact a thinking, feeling being. I like to think the pecan pie sits there expectantly, and happy, because there is always hope that it will make someone utterly happy with its whole, and even if someone eats some of its pieces, it has more, until it's gone, and once it's gone, it means someone, somewhere was like, "Fuck yeah, pecan pie, num num

num." Even if the pie doesn't think and feel those things, I'm better than a piece of pie. I have the choice to wrap the people up who don't like me in my trash bag full of things I don't give a shit about anymore, and throw them out. Fine, don't eat me. Someone, somewhere, is going to love my whole. Even if someone takes pieces from me, I will still have something left. I'll just have to give out servings with a little more discernment, so I can find the one who decides I'm the best they've ever tried, so much so, they want to know my recipe, so they can make more.

In the meantime, I will keep adding ingredients to my whole, through learning, reading, watching, listening, running, and creating, and even losing.

Ugh, this is getting intense what with the pie metaphors. But hey, this is my book.

The constant through all this is that my tattoo pieces help me make up the world I choose to live in. They are for me, for my own heart, for my own eyes and for my own healing. I look at them when the world has turned ugly. They give me beauty as I discover a new line every time I look at them.

My most recent tattoo of a rose grew from the disintegration of the longest romantic relationship of my life. That time was grotesque and it's still ongoing. I had run out of tears to cry anymore and all felt lost. It was once again time to fill back up on hope. I poured myself back into a black leather chair and I let an excited artist pack my forearm with deep reds and subdued greens. I injected my body with pain and ink on purpose, of my own choice. The physical hurt created more color in my world one more time. I know that space will be a place I can always return to when I feel empty. I eat that shit up.

# Jesus Vs. Santa

Religion has always been spotty in my life, and quite frankly, I've depended on my period more times than I have religion to get me out of a jam. I sought faith out, I really did. I searched for spirituality, enlightenment, faith in something, anything, all things. It usually only lasted for a couple hours at a time though.

When I was little, I watched my dad pray before every single meal, even if it was served on a wobbly TV tray, which it most often was. He brought his hands to his face, touching them together in prayer, and his usually large looking hands seemed small. I remember seeing streaks of gray in his black curls as he bowed his head. He swayed back and forth, mumbled something, then crossed himself and eventually shoveled food into his mouth. He ate more avocados with every meal than all the Millennials put together on this planet, before avocados were cool. I think it was a Puerto Rican thing.

It was strange to me that a raging alcoholic was so devoted to a God that never helped him put down the beer. I mean, what kind of guardian angel didn't just straight knock him on his ass after he downed a shooter of whiskey in the upstairs bathroom. Dad thought he was slick by hiding them under toilet paper in the trashcan. We all knew the empty bottles were there, but we just didn't talk about them.

When I was young, we lived in New Jersey during the single time I remember Dad assaulting mom. My memory ultimately fails me. As I remember it, I burst into my parents' bedroom because I could hear muffled cries and yells from mom. Mom says I was in my crib in their bedroom while they fought.

The bedroom had always meant naptime to me before this. When I thought of it, I thought of mom carrying me in and placing me on her bed. The curtains let a golden glow into the bedroom, and were patterned in a forest of dark green trees. The shitty apartment didn't matter, because that bedroom was home. It was warm, it was golden, it was the smell of mom's hair.

The night of the fight the room was stark bright. I remember flashes of angry strobe light instead of the orange glow. Mom and dad were facing each other, squared off. She was so small, he wasn't tall but he stood towering over her in only the way a father can. I don't remember the words he hurled at her, just the sounds. Dad had his hands raised, choking air instead of her neck.

As I remember it, I ran in front of mom and pointed my tiny little finger up at dad, as he continued screaming at her. The way mom tells it, I just screamed and cried in my crib.

"You leave mommy alone!" I yelled at dad.

"No Laura, go in the other room honey, please go," said mom as she pushed me out of the way.

I don't know how the fight ended or what stopped it, let alone what started it. We'll call it booze for funsies sake.

At some point, I found myself sitting on mom's lap, as she talked to a detective at the police department.

I stretched my neck so I could look at her face, to make sure she was still there with me. Her bottom lip was crusted and purple, with blood and bruising. It felt like I was sitting on a washing machine, as her body shook and her voice trembled as she talked. She placed her hand on my cheek and forced my face forward, away from hers.

"Don't look at mommy honey," she told me.

"I don't want him to go to jail, I don't want anything bad to happen to him," mom told the detective. It was like episodes of a crime TV show, the woman insisting the man not be punished, not because she loved him, but because he was the one who made the money and the family couldn't afford for the dipshit to miss work.

I don't remember the drive home. I must have fallen asleep.

The next morning, I was playing out on the front porch when I looked up the street and saw dad coming up the sidewalk. His brown jacket slung over his shoulder as he shuffled up the stairs. I had no idea he had been in jail the previous night.

I once found cigarettes in mom's purse and automatically bawled my eyes out because only bad people smoked, so mom must be bad. I don't know what I would have thought about dad had I known he had been locked up. I'd seen enough episodes of COPS to know bad guys should be avoided at all costs and officers deserved awards for dealing with drunken people who swear they hadn't had anything to drink that night.

I knew I should be mad at dad, but for what, I wasn't sure. I knew he had something to do with why mom was so sad, but at that age I hadn't put beer and liquor together to equal spousal abuse.

I let him hug me and then felt bad, because I hugged him back, and meant it.

Dad eventually stopped hitting mom, mostly because when I was in fifth grade we moved from New Jersey to Indiana. We moved into a house right next door to my grandparents and Grandpa's shotguns served as insurance against dad beating on mom anymore. I have a feeling dad's prayers changed to a common theme of, "Dear God, please keep Grandpa Jim from shooting me today, thank you, Amen."

Mom doesn't believe in God these days. Can't say I blame her. I think the saddest part is she doesn't even want to look anymore. She was Baptist as a kid, but then converted to Catholicism, the same sect where dad grew up with the guilt of religion his entire life, so maybe that's why the drink got to him. I said 'the drink,' I sound like a 60-year-old-woman.

Maybe dad talked to God so much because he needed it more than most, because he caused so much pain. Maybe he had so much more to say and apologize for, like the time he hit mom so hard in the side of her head that she still has hearing problems to this day. Maybe he had to apologize for the prostitutes and cocaine use.

Once I reached high school, I tried going to church. I joined a youth group and bought into everything. I scrounged all week, just to have a couple bucks to add to the collection plate because I couldn't bring myself to ask my parents for the money. I watched my best friend, Katie, get baptized and I even played Mary in the Christmas shenanigans. When the preacher asked every week who wanted to be saved, I'd start to sweat, knowing I should raise my hand, but I could never do it. I wasn't much for dunking my head under water.

The youth group leaders, Anne and Brad, were a young married couple who had been trying to have a baby, with no luck. They were at the church to mentor us and teach us about the everlasting love of Jesus. Eventually, Brad's sister-in-law, Sarah, became pregnant and the whole congregation celebrated, still a little sad for Anne because she still was without a child.

Apparently though, Brad had been spending a little too much prayer time with Sarah, his sister-in-law, and her baby was his, and not his brother's. I know, I know, it's getting kind of Game of Throney up in here.

I never went back to that church.

A redheaded freckled girl, Red, we'll call her, saved me in gym class one day. Red always wore long skirts, except in gym class, in gym class she wore culottes and yes I had to look up how to spell culottes and I question even using the word because I suspect a lot of people won't remember the culottes phenomenon in the 90's. I never understood Red's justification for wearing skirts all the time because I asked her why she didn't wear pants, and she told me it was because pants were clothes of men and she was a woman, but then I stated, "Well, Jesus most definitely wore a dress, so that makes no fucking sense." Somehow we were still friends.

Little did I know, a few years later, Red would steal my first love from me, but not really because he was probably never really mine, as he wasn't a sweater and I can't actually own a human being.

In high school, there on the basketball courts Red held my hands and made me say a bunch of stuff I was supposed to be sorry for.

I said, "I know I'm a sinner, and a dirty little shit, not fit to walk in His Kingdom, but through the grace of Jesus, I am saved, Hallelujah." I looked up and screamed "Christ!" for good measure and immediately felt like I needed to take a bath for being so dirty, you know, from the sin.

That weekend, Red convinced me that taking a ride in her church's white school bus out to a compound of trailers was a good idea. I think she was Baptist, but when I say Baptist, I mean the kind where 9-year-olds speak in tongues and wave handkerchiefs in the air as the preacher tells you, you're going to hell. I was slightly terrified and grossly confused. The little girl next to me was ghost white and blonde to the point that now I'm pretty sure she was Albino. I mean, there's nothing wrong with being an Albino, unless you're a 70-year-old in a kid's body and you speak in tongues. I feared some geezer was going to soul suck me and I'd never get the chance to have sex. I thought,

"What the shit, I was under the impression Red over there saved me last week during a game of dodge ball, and now this preacher is still telling me I'm going to hell. There better not be any fucking snakes either."

The people in charge of the congregation said us girls, had to split up from the adults and boys to have the youth lesson of the week.

I filed into a separate trailer and sat in a folding chair with roughly ten other teenagers. The Leader Lady put on a video clip of a popular adult cartoon with really obscene kid characters in it. It was an episode where Jesus fights Satan. She then played another clip where Jesus and Santa fight via video game tactics in a mall, slaughtering bystanders. I officially lost my shit. I looked around and realized I was the only one laughing among the other teens. I turned red as the Leader Lady went on a tirade about how evil TV shows are today and how dare they pit Jesus against Satan and Santa. All the other teens agreed that Santa was in fact evil and Jesus would obviously win in a real fight. Because you know, if there was one talent Jesus had, it was fisticuffs.

I furrowed my brow, trying to figure out how the hell I was going to get out of the little trailer with Corn People all around me. I'm pretty sure I was chastised some more for laughing because, obviously, I couldn't stop, even twenty minutes after the lesson.

Eventually I made it home and said fuck that, never again.

The next weekend, the white bus stopped in front of my house and two kids knocked on my door to see if I was coming back.

"No, I'm sorry, I actually already belong to another church," I said.

"Oh really, what church?" they asked in unison.

"Uh, the Tabernacle of Sister St. Mary and Alma, Check Your Battery!" I yelled. Then I slammed the door shut and went back to bed.

I guess my childhood didn't really foster a great religious experience. I again dove into attempted transcendence in college. I read about various religions; Hinduism, The Tao Te Ching a Ling a Ding, the Benediction pre Cumbersomebatch, Buddhism. I half-heartedly tried meditation, and then there was my favorite, the Tao of Poo, the overeating bear.

Nothing stuck.

Well, nothing really stuck until one six-hour drive to Missouri from Indiana for Army duties. I did what I often did on long drives; thought about the past, how much I'd messed things up, how – alone I really was, even when I had a boyfriend, wah wah, that kind of stuff. There were no less than three sobbing episodes along the way.

I was driving on my fifth hour in, and for some reason, I was tired of feeling sad, so, naturally I thought about a scene in the movie Rush Hour, the scene where the little girl is sitting in the back of a car, singing along to a Mariah Carey song. The little girl belted out the lyrics while her bodyguard, played by Jackie Chan, grimaced. He loved her like his own so he let her sing.

There was no particular reason to think of that scene in that particular moment. I hadn't seen the movie for nearly a decade.

I was aching to hear the same song from the movie. I love me some Mariah Carey. I whined as I changed the static channels ever present on highway drives. Also, explain to me why the only stations that come in on the radio during long drives are religious talk shows, they come in crystal fucking clear. Coincidence? I think not.

I hit the seek button and waited for something good to come on. Then I heard it.

*(Legally, I could totally put the lyrics here, but in an effort to Weird Al it and show my age, I tweaked the words and I realize maybe only the diehard fans will know what song I'm talking about, but here goes.)*

"OH WHEN YOU STROLL BY EVVVERY NIGHT, WHISPERING TWEETS AND LOOKING PRIME…" I heard on the radio.

"Shut the front door!" I screamed at no one. My effing song was playing. I know, there's a lot of yelling and screaming in this book, welcome to my life.

"IMAGES OF CRAPSHOOTS, CREEP INTO ME FULLY, AS YOU BITE INTO MY BREEAADD…AND MY ARTERIES BEAT FASTER, WHEN YOU TAKE MEOWHHH-VER, TIME AND TIME AND TIME BEEHIVVE," the diva sang over the sound waves.

I just shook my head, wiggled in my seat and enjoyed the ride.

Then God said, "Here's looking at you kid." Then I said, "Nope, still not buying it!"

# The Jiggen' is Burning

I graduated from the Army's Advanced Individual Training in October of 2006. I had gone through three months of demonically hard tasks in order to serve my country. I was officially a Military Police Officer, well, for one weekend a month, two weeks a year that is. Graduation was the best day of my life, only in the fact that it would mean a void of feeling miserable every second of the day. My grandparents and mom came to see me in Fort Leonard Wood, Missouri, on my big day.

To commemorate the accomplishment, we went to Branson, Missouri, or as others call it, little Nashville. Mom told me dad said he was sorry he couldn't make it on the trip, but he had to work. In Branson, we watched shows like small versions of Cirque de Soleil and a very entertaining water and lights show. I also got lost on a run. I had gone out that morning on my own, only to realize I didn't know how to get back to the hotel. I had to call my grandpa to come get me…so much for learning land navigation from the Army.

"Ok, where are you?" my grandpa asked over the phone.

"I don't know where I'm at, hence why I don't know how to get to where you are Grandpa!" I cried over the phone. It only took about forty minutes for him to find me on the side of the road, dripping wet from a rainstorm. I had gone on the run because I was still deathly afraid of losing my fitness level by being lazy and felt like I had to work out constantly to be combat ready. Lord I was misinformed on how my enlistment was going to go.

At one show, I got to dance on a stage with Lionel Richie. Well it wasn't actually him, but an impersonator. I can say Lionel was thoroughly impressed with my moves as I butt bumped him to the beat of "All Night Long." Also, a very convincing version of the Blues Brothers and Elvis sang directly to me. Elvis even wrapped a blue sash around my shoulders as he crooned to me. All the attention probably had something to do with the fact that I was the youngest person in the audience at any given time and I had a vagina.

Once the sites were seen and the trip was ending, we drove the few hours home to Indiana. We picked up fast food on the way. Dad was happy to see me and gave me a hug when I walked into the house. I lugged in my three duffel bags and some other family members were there. I received my hugs and kisses, then I plopped down to eat.

I sat at a TV tray in the living room, chowing down on some fries, when I noticed everyone seemed to gather in the living room. They stood around rather awkwardly, looking at me, while being very quiet. Mom muted the TV and took a deep breath.

"You remember we told you dad couldn't come on the trip because he had to work?" mom asked.

"Yeah," I said, eyes unblinking. His absence hadn't come as a shock. Despite the years of chaos, booze, and fits, dad always had a job no matter if it was in a factory, at a mall, or a donut store. He did whatever he had to do to feed us.

At that time, he had worked at a pawnshop as a jeweler. He said they kept him around because he could speak Spanish. I had trouble swallowing my fries.

I looked at mom as she talked and knew something was wrong. The conversation was muddy and heavy, reeking of something I didn't want to hear.

"Well, Laura, that wasn't entirely the truth," she said. She kept talking and I just kept dipping my fries in ketchup. I heard a few words here and there.

"Cancer….chest…lungs….everywhere…going to do radiation…won't work…few months…best not to tell you…you were going through so much," she said. Dad was nowhere to be found. Not that I remember anyways. He was probably outside in the garage, smoking weed, because you know, that was what kept him eating.

I took a bite of my chicken sandwich and everything turned blurry and distorted with tears, but I still chewed. I asked a few questions, but was only told, "We don't know." I went to bed thinking everything was fine. He would be fine, I thought, nothing would kill that son-of-a-bitch. He had already had a liver transplant a couple years prior and he had made it through that.

Before the transplant, dad had started pissing blood and doctors said he had cirrhosis of the liver. Alcoholism isn't very glamorous, despite what the commercials tell you about having the time of your life. Oh sure, Heineken likes to claim that "Heineken refreshes the parts other beers cannot reach," and if by saying refreshing, they meant eroding bodily organs that water couldn't reach, then fuck yeah, they were right, as he eventually needed a liver transplant. Dad went to AA, God apparently had some things to say to him and he stopped drinking. I wouldn't say that when he stopped drinking it made him a nicer person. It just made him quieter.

After about a year on the transplant list, a little black beeper gave him another chance at life. Someone else died, and he got her liver. He craved jellybeans after that, or maybe I made the jellybean thing up. When I went to the hospital to see him after the surgery, all I could see was the scar. I don't remember what he was hooked up to, I just remember the jagged gash, sewn up, splitting his skin from the top of his stomach to the bottom and all the way across, like Frankenstein's monster full of stitches. It was grotesque and I was scared to look at the raw flesh. That day, dad looked like a fairytale monster, instead of his usual uncanny likeness to Saddam Hussein, the real life monster, mustache and all.

When mom told me dad had cancer I told myself this whole thing was just a blip, he'd already almost died, no one ever goes through life and almost dies twice. I then went about my life, going on hospital trips with my parents. I thought it would all blow over soon and dad would go back to being himself, an asshole who never said the right thing or picked up after himself.

A month or so later, I checked in with the Army unit I had been assigned. I sat in the administrative office with a few military people who were a hell of a lot nicer than my drill sergeants had been. Maybe this wouldn't be so bad, I thought.

Then, a blonde woman in uniform came into the office in a huff.

"I got pulled over on the way here," she said. "I tried to tell him we were deploying soon, but the asshole still gave me a speeding ticket."

So, I was going to be going to Iraq in a few months. Well would you look at that, I thought. My recruiter didn't lie about that at least. He always said, it wasn't a matter of if I would be deployed, just a matter of when.

Even more months later, I was in Texas, training in all the ways to be a prison guard for Iraqi detainees. It was awful, it was long, but it kept me busy.

Towards the end of the training, I was riding on a bus from a shopping trip at the Post Exchange back to our living quarters and I got a phone call. We had about a week left before we were allowed to go home for four days, then we'd ship out to Iraq for good. I was told once I got back to the barracks, I needed to come to the First Sergeant's office.

"Oh shit, what did I do?" I asked my bus mate sitting next to me.

You usually only have to see the First Sergeant if you've either royally fucked something up, or if you've done something amazing, and I sure as shit hadn't done anything amazing.

I went to see First Sergeant Scott, and he looked apprehensive, not mean, which was not good.

"How you doing Bonano?" Scott asked.

"I'm good First Sergeant," I said, standing at parade rest, with my feet hip width apart and arms clasped behind my back.

"Relax," he said, meaning I could stand like a normal human being. "You received a Red Cross message, your father has been moved to hospice care, we're going to put you on pass early so you can go home."

"Yes First Sergeant," I said quietly.

I stared down at the papers he had on his desk, but couldn't tell you what any of them said because I wasn't seeing them. I simply existed in a space I did not want to exist in. My sensations weren't internal; they were all on the outside. My uniform felt tight and scratchy on my skin, my cheeks were hot because he was looking at me expectantly and I wasn't reacting the way he thought I should.

"This doesn't seem to upset you, you not close with your dad?" he asked.

"He's been sick for awhile, we knew it was coming First Sergeant," I said. He then dismissed me to go pack. I had wanted to tell him my dad was a piece of shit. I'd wanted to say, "My dad was an awful man who abused my mother, he drank and smoked and smacked and kicked and spit. He cussed and called mom a skunk bitch more times than I think he told her he loved her," I wanted to say. I wanted to tell him my dad always called me a whore, so one day I finally just went ahead and became a whore to prove him right.

Grandpa once told me about a conversation he had with dad before dad got really sick. Dad was in the garage, head down, working on jewelry like he always did. His boss let him do a lot of his work at home in the garage, where he built up his own shop full of lamps and machines and magic.

"How you doing Al?" grandpa asked, walking into the garage. He said dad's eyes glistened when he looked up from his hands.

"How the fuck do you think I'm doing, Jim?" dad asked. "I'm fucking dying."

But I didn't tell the First Sergeant any of that.

On the trip home from Texas, I got thoroughly drunk for free. I met a perfectly nice couple at an airport bar and they bought me many rounds of drinks as I told them my sob story and they told me about their long-distance relationship. I wonder if they made it down the road together and get to look upon each other's faces now every morning.

When I got home to Indiana, mom picked me up from the airport and told me how things had been since I'd left. They had gotten a hospital bed and put it in the living room for dad because he couldn't walk up the stairs anymore. They brought in a special toilet seat stand so he could go to the bathroom, but it didn't help enough. They knew they had to move him to hospice when mom found dad in the kitchen, on his hands and knees, cleaning up his own shit because he couldn't hold his bowels anymore. Mom found him wiping the mess off the black linoleum flooring, cursing and panicking.

I thought back to the time dad had installed that black linoleum. Mom had been so happy he had done it for her. After it was finished and she was smiling he lightly tapped her butt and she swatted his hand away. Later, maybe a week or so, dad had been cooking on the stove and caught a pot lid on fire, the glass broke and melted a spot on the floor.

"Laowra!" dad yelled. "The jiggen is burning, the jiggen is burning!" he screamed as he ran from the stove to the sink and back again. I ran in, grabbed a chair so I could reach the screeching fire alarm. I couldn't possibly deal with a catastrophe with so much noise.

"What?" I screamed, "What did you do dad?" I couldn't understand him.

I let his phrase, "The jiggen is burning," sink in and realized what he meant. The chicken, the chicken was burning, not the jiggen. This wasn't anything out of the ordinary really. Dad had a lot of issues with fire in our lifetime together and the side of our garage has never been the same since he melted it while trying to grill hotdogs many summers ago.

Fast-forward a millennium. The radiation hadn't worked, so they moved him into hospice.

I don't know, call me crazy, but I kind of feel like hospice is a cruel trick. It's basically saying, "Meh, maybe don't have any more hope cause you're going to die." They say, "Look, we'll make it more comfortable and give you lots of pamphlets about dying. Oh, and morphine, we'll give you so much morphine you won't even WANT to find a reason to live anymore."

Once I made it back to Indiana, sobered up after a nap, mom and I made it to the hospital and she warned me that dad had been given a lot of pain meds the last few days, but they made sure to decrease it because they knew I was coming.

He was dozing when I slipped up to the bed and leaned over his face so he could see me. His eyes opened wide, along with his mouth, but he couldn't talk very well. He let out a low moan and raised his arms to me, shaking his head in excitement.

I'd never seen joy like that in his face when he looked at me before. Not when I graduated from college, or preschool for that matter, not when I told him I was engaged, not when we danced salsa at some party, not even when I told him I was joining the Army. Actually, when I told him I was deploying, he was upset.

We stood out on the back porch, the one he had built with his own hands. We were under the stars, our breath covering the dotted lights in the sky with cloudy mist.

"Oh Laura, this was the stupidest thing you could have ever done," he said. "You shouldn't have joined. But I'll tell 'ju what, ju hear a loud noise, ju run, ju keep your head down. Don't turn jour back to anyone either, they'll stab ju."

I told him this wasn't Vietnam. This was the 21st Century. I'd just be guarding prisoners and I'd be safe with them behind bars, or wires, or something. Little did I know, I would often have to sit alone in a tiny room with six detainees, awaiting their court proceedings to see if they would be released or not. I never did turn my back to them though.

In his hospital bed, dad's mouth formed into the biggest smile I knew his decaying body was capable of, which wasn't much. It was everything to me. I don't think he knew I was coming to see him. He put his thin arms around me and hugged me, a weightless hug. He had wasted away to a skeleton, cheeks sunken, face gray, not the beautiful brown it had always been. The skin was peeling off of his lips. I think I slept at the hospital that night.

A couple days later, mom took me to a shitty franchise restaurant to get away from the hospital for a little bit. I ordered my food, sirloin steak, sweet potato fries, and a beer on a weekday afternoon. I was mad at the sun for shining, there were people dying, and yet the sun still shined in my eyes through the blinds.

Minutes later, the waiter came up to us looking concerned and said, "I'm very sorry, but it's Election Day and we shouldn't have served you that beer." I cocked my head, thought about chugging it, but handed it off. Fuck me right.

The next few days just happened. Now, I look at pictures someone took from that time and it makes no sense. Snapping pictures of people in the bottom of sadness seems wrong. Sadness and the face of a man not there anymore in the pictures, his eyes blank, sucked dry from the drugs.

The day the news came that dad's mother wouldn't be coming from New York, was the beginning of the end. The hospital staff had stopped feeding him food because the cancer just fed on it. It would just prolong things, the nurse said. Instead, mom gave him water from a little green straw sponge. She mostly just wiped his lips with it. He begged to go outside to smoke a cigarette.

During one of his lucid moments, the nurse was at his bedside, talking to him, because obviously they were friends now.

"Hey, hey, give me jour number," dad asked the nurse. She laughed.

"Really dad, I'm right here, I can hear you hitting on the nurse," I told him through giggles.

I don't know what day it was, but at some point, in 2007, the female Chaplain came to dad's room. He had been gasping more and more for breath as the day wore on. He rattled and wheezed and I wished he would just stop. The Chaplain was Catholic maybe, but I'm not sure because I'm pretty sure women can't be Catholic Priests, so to me, she was a Priestess, with a purple sash. It reminded me of the blue sash Elvis had given me in Branson. I was sitting in the corner as she stood over him, we all lowered our heads and hushed words were spoken as he confessed his sins, I suppose. I wish I had listened better to his Last Rite.

Shortly after that, a nurse put something in his IV, she said it would make it easier for him to go. He was suffering.

I soon fell asleep on the maroon plastic couch in the hospital room.

I awoke to mom shaking me, telling me it was time. I lurched upright, but didn't stand up. I didn't move to him. I didn't take my eyes off of him, and I didn't count how many times he rasped in and out for air, in a moment he just didn't anymore. I felt everyone else in the room inhale, waiting for another of his exhalations to come, but it didn't. Someone cried out. Then his chest moved one more time and froth came out of his mouth, and he was still. I know I cried, I just don't remember it.

I don't know what I expected death to feel like. This was it though, I guessed.

Mom scooted up next to him on the bed and rubbed his forehead. She was tiny beside him. She told him she loved him, and I thought of all the times she had said in the past she hoped he would die, even when he wasn't even sick yet. I wasn't mad at her though. He did that to her. The years of him showing her she didn't matter made her say that. But she took care of him when he did get sick. She was there for every second of every day of his pain, unfortunately, it was hers too.

Then I remembered when I was little, and would run up to him chirping, "Swing me daddy swing me." I'd then turn around with my back to him, and he'd grab me under the arms, pull me between his legs and launch me forward into the air, over and over. One day I ran up to him, in our small kitchen in New Jersey, singing, but he said he couldn't swing me anymore, his back hurt too much. That was a sad day.

About an hour later, in the hospital, maybe less, everyone filed out of his room and I stayed to say goodbye.

It was like a stranger lying in the bed in his place. I couldn't smell the Vidal Sassoon hair cream anymore, or the Stetson cologne he usually bought at the grocery store. I hesitantly touched his arm. It was dry, not cold yet. I said I was sorry, for what, I didn't know, I was just sorry. I kissed him, and I might have felt his mustache on my cheek, or imagined it, I don't know if they had shaved it off. I always hated it when he shaved his mustache. He wasn't dad without it. I stepped back from the bed, but then had to walk forward again. I couldn't force myself to leave, until I did.

I never saw him again, except in a dream I had after he died. In my dream, he swung me, but this time, I was facing him and could see his face. That was a good dream.

I flew back to Texas the day after he died. Dad's funeral was to be on the day my unit flew to Iraq. I didn't see him buried because I wanted to make the trip with my unit along with people I knew, rather than catching a later flight, alone.

I never liked the smell of funeral flowers anyway.

# Roots of My Tree

I've never met most of my dad's family. Adalberto Bonano, or Al as everyone called him, is still a stranger to me. I only know he was born in Rio Grande, Puerto Rico, lived in Fajardo and San Juan, and grew up in a neighborhood that had tin roofs, and possibly dirt floors. For fun as a kid, my dad and his friends would hang out on a hill and throw rocks onto the houses to shake and rattle a person's afternoon. I'm sure he probably got an ass beating here or there for that.

Another fun activity for him was to grab onto the tails of cows, giving them a whap on their rears as he held on for dear life as the cows ran through the mud. Ironically, mom later married a man from India and I have a feeling he would have been none too happy to hear about this pastime, considering the sacredness of bovines in Indian culture.

I like to imagine what my dad was like as he'd play with his brothers and sisters, he was one of five children of his parents, Gregoria and Augustin.

One day, a man approached my dad and his friend and asked them if they wanted to learn something. Most kids should probably scream no and run away, but what the hell, they said yes. The man taught them the alchemy of metals and jewels and dad became a jeweler.

Eventually, Al moved to New York. How he met my mom in Indiana, I'm not sure. He said he liked her legs; they danced, and were married soon after. For some time, mom, dad, and my brother Jamie lived in Ohio, then Arizona, then eventually New Jersey. I was born. A few years later mom whispered to me that I'd have a little brother or sister soon. The baby never came. Mom arrived home from the doctor, eyes red and said I wouldn't have a new brother or sister after all. Apparently, miscarriages are a trend in my family, but mom and dad kept trying. Shortly after, a baby boy was born. They called him Ricardo. Meanwhile dad took the bus from New Jersey to New York for work.

Al worked for a Hasidic Jewish man and had, what I thought, was the most glamorous job I'd ever imagined. His work area was on a top floor, with a giant window spanning an entire wall space. You could see the city, the smog and cars, and it was beautiful in a dirty kind of way only New York can be. The noise from outside was turned silent as his machinery hummed and buzzed.

Sometimes, dad would bring me to work with him and I'd get angry because he'd make me ride in a stroller along the streets to get there. I remember thinking I was too old for a stroller and thought strangers were laughing at me. Dad would bring me into the office, plop me in a chair, and dump a pile of emeralds on a table in front of me.

"Laura, you have to take the ones that look like dees," he'd say and hold a single one up for me to look at, "and put them in a pile. Take the ones that look dees way, into another pile." God knows I probably had thousands of dollars' worth of jewels sitting in front of me, but it didn't occur to me to pocket even one, just one wouldn't be missed. Alas, I was a kid and had no concept of how many Cabbage Patch Dolls I could buy with just one of those deep and dark stones. I just liked sorting them. That might be the start of my enjoyment of sorting things. Mom had a giant tin of various buttons; pastel ones that were milky with stripes going through them, shiny silver ones, bulbous gold ones. I'd pile similar ones together, only to just dump them back into the tin once I was finished sorting. Apparently, this is a phenomenon that happens worldwide, as I've heard stories of others doing this, yet here I was, thinking I was special.

When we walked through the city to the bus station, dad seemed at home. He could cross streets in front of cars like no one else. I think New York was always where his heart was. I think the smells and sounds gave him something to wake up for. He lived for buying a guy on the street a hot dog from a steaming and umbrella'd hot dog stand, only zesty mustard at the ready. I think everyone's life has a signature melody. His was a mixture of a salsa band, trumpeting and hollering, but then it decided to break into jazz at some point. First, fiery and booming, then lowering to humming stanzas going all over the place, until it quiets down and starts all over. New York is a lot like that. I think Indiana lowered the volume of his life a little.

Once a year in Indiana, we would get a post card or letter from dad's friend, Javier who also became a jeweler. They would come from far places I'd never heard of, Barbados, Venezuela. Javier's life stayed loud.

On one of our daddy-daughter days at his work, dad told me he was taking me on a train. I squealed with anticipation, took his hand (HA, no stroller this day), followed him through a subway platform, and held onto a silver bar as the train we got on rocked. I stood there, small and significant in my own place, imagining how much fun riding on a train would be. It smelled like pee. I'd hoped we'd get a stage car to ourselves. We got off and dad asked if I liked the train.

I scowled at him.

"But we haven't gotten on the train yet," I said.

He laughed and said we had, we had just then stepped off of the train. It had not been at all what I'd expected, what we just did was gross and gloomy I thought. This was only the first lesson I'd learn about the idea of expectation vs. reality.

We lived in Indiana when the Towers fell.

That day at school, I walked into my English class, the TV was on and I thought, "Oh boy, we're watching a movie, best day ever." It was turned to the news though; the first tower was smoking and the sky was a hazy dull blue on the screen. My teenage brain had no intention of grasping what it all meant. The newscast bled into my next class, Political Science, where the only word I remember hearing was 'war.' I went home and went about my business, did my homework, completely blind to the fact that so many were forever changed that day. I had no idea the pain the people felt as they were thrust into history, no idea of the terror as they jumped, they burned and suffocated, were crushed, and flew to their deaths. I'm ashamed of my then young heart and how little it felt at the time.

Dad came home from work and I walked into the living room to see him. He was sitting in front of the TV, on the edge of the velvety recliner.

I'd never seen my dad cry before.

When I say cry I mean he sobbed, his face soaked, eyes clenched closed, not wanting to see what was happening. He shook his fist at the television, rocked and grabbed at his face, head, chest, and heart. I stood beside him, my hands at my side because I didn't know what to do with them.

"Those sons-of bitches…oh my God… look what those bastards did…so many," he screamed at the screen. At the time, I didn't know who 'those bastards' were, terrorism wasn't in my vocabulary yet, but I could see dad hated them for what they did. Distraught, he slapped his thigh over and over, still crying. Mom probably told him to calm down. To this day, mom still thinks Amish and Jewish people are one in the same, I'm not sure she understood what happened that day either.

I imagine that when my dad watched the Towers fall in New York, it was like watching his own tribe burn, and he couldn't do anything to stop it. He probably had more memories from that home than any other in his life.

A week later, my friend Jon joined the Army, setting in motion years later, my eventual enlistment. I joined the Army a week after Jon was killed by an IED in Iraq in

2005. When our bombs initially hit Baghdad, I wrote in my journal that night the news said we were going to war. The dark footage of the air strike was grainy and glowed green. Buildings occasionally lit up in bright balls every now and then. I had no idea at the time, I'd become a part of that war.

Regrets are rarely useful in life, but I regret I never fell to my dad's feet that day and that I never hugged him. I didn't even say I was sorry for what he felt. My memories of New York were of the night dad brought home a skinny white kitten in a wet brown box. He said he had found it in the alley behind his building. I fell in love with its blue eyes, but it wasn't meant to be. Mom made us get rid of it. It was probably long gone by the time the Towers fell though.

We didn't lose any family or friends that day, but they were dad's people. I'd wondered if years ago, he could have crossed paths with at least one person in that city who didn't make it home that day from the stairwells. Where his building was in relation to the Towers, I didn't know. The world is never as big as it seemed in the past, once heartache hits.

Another place dad acted at ease was at Aunt Carmen's apartment in New Jersey, or was it New York? I'm not sure where it was, but that's neither here nor there. Her home felt more like an island all on its own.

Carmen was like a caricature of a real person. She was large and the space she took up oozed joy. She had the loudest and deepest laugh I've ever heard and she did it with her whole body, hands clapping, shoulders shaking.

She would reach out with her large fingers, with manicured long nails, to grasp others to her as she laughed. She always wore lipstick, a purple red that never smeared. She always looked glamorous even when her head was wrapped in a scarf, her bronze-brown skin smooth and dewed from sweat that always smelled sweet, with a hint of cigarette smoke. I didn't even mind it when she'd squeeze my face in her palms.

"Que linda," she would coo to me when I was small. Dad often packed us all up to visit her and those visits made me see color when most of life was muted.

Her apartment looked like a stage set from an off-Broadway play with a shitty budget, but somehow it worked. It gave off a warm glow that smelled like cleaning powder and she'd feed me galletas de soda, or soda crackers from a shiny emerald green tin, which was the closest she could get to casabe bread.

Her matriarch melody was of a smooth Latin Lounge, and I have vague memories of music always playing in the background around her with the lights dimmed orange. I could only catch words of "Por la vida … porque … Lalalala…and tu Corazon," among the horns and guitars. A black velvet painting hung above her couch. A splayed matador had gouged a bull and the bull leaked a neon pink line of blood that looked like a child had drawn it with a crayon. The matador had such pretty socks, I always thought. But I always felt bad for the bull, what had it done to deserve being stabbed by a fancy man?

I was always hungry at Carmen's apartment because of the aroma of her cooking; it smelled of cocina criolla, Yuca, salty olives, cilantro, onions, garlic and the holy grail of Puerto Rican spices, Adobo. Carmen didn't just cook though, she swayed her hips and swirled whatever spoon she had in one hand, a beer in the other, as she fried tostones, or plantains. To this day, I still can't get sofrito right. My favorite was a beef stew with red beans, tomato sauce, olives, carrots, and potatoes. Carmen was a Boricua goddess, if I'd ever met one. Statuesque, she was dad's only sibling I ever really knew. Dad's mother had lost all five of her children before she died.

I think I'd always been jealous of my half-sister Angie, because she resembled Carmen in a way I never would. Tall and brown with curves she wasn't ashamed of. Angie had feminine guiles I never learned, boys literally waiting outside of her window when she came to visit us. I would borrow Angie's high heels and try to walk in them. She got mad at me when I scuffed her bright white pumps.

I don't know where I was in my life when mom told me over the phone one day that Carmen had died. She had suffered from epilepsy and I had always known it was a terrible and scary thing to have. I once saw Carmen have a seizure on the front porch stairs and didn't understand that someone could choke on their own vomit. Carmen shook and I could only see the whites of her eyes as she fell back on the steps and I remember being very scared. I don't know if an ambulance came or not that day, but she had survived that one. The day she died, she had no one with her at her apartment to help her.

I imagine she looked beautiful at her funeral, graceful and alive even in her stillness.

There have only been a few times in my life I've felt the pride of the stock I come from. I do think I have a slight advantage in dancing. My hips pop and sway in a somewhat more natural way than most non-Hispanic girls. I have an aversion to pumpkin spice anything, so that's a plus. When I go to my local ethnic grocery store, the cashiers speak to me in Spanish, and at first, I'm excited.

"They like me, they really like me…they think I'm one of them," I say to myself. But then I have to say, "Lo siento, I can't understand you por qué un pequeño Español…el, dónde está el baño?" and after five years of taking Spanish in school, I don't think I'm any better off than if I hadn't taken it at all.

For the times I curse my thick curly hair, I honestly wouldn't want any other crown of glory. It's crazy and frizzy sometimes, but sometimes, just sometimes, it bounces just right and spirals into tendrils that people say they want to murder me for, so I got that going for me. So what if people confuse me as Asian, it's a total mind blow, an Asian with curly hair. I just tell them I'm Hawaiian. I didn't get the tan from dad either, but that's ok, it tried soaking through in the form of freckles. Freckles hide wrinkles so that's another win for me. And my butt, my butt is amazing.

# When Did This Happen?

In 2015, I was in a daily meeting while deployed to Afghanistan and I came to a ridiculous conclusion that almost knocked the breath out of me. It was a day I knew was coming, but it hit me hard.

At 31-years-old, I was a grownup.

I sat there at the meeting surrounded by other Soldiers and grown ass people. I was adulting and saying things an adult would say, but I felt ridiculous. When the shit did this happen? My main boss on the deployment, Marie, was also one of my best friends. I sat and looked at her in awe as she was all authoritative and scary. In the past, I'd spent countless nights out dancing with her, and other nights crying on her, and even more times laughing on her.

Let's backtrack to my days of being carefree and very un-adult like. We had deployed together in 2007 to Iraq and we made it home without a scratch. A few days after the unit came home after the 15-month deployment, the higher ups decided to let us party it up at a local Veterans of Foreign Wars establishment in El Paso. Marie wasn't allowed to drink because she wasn't 21 yet. The rest of us drank and passed her secret sips of ours. I found it completely odd and irrational that she had been old enough to go to a combat zone, had the potential of being killed or kill someone else, but in the good old U.S. of A. she wasn't considered old enough to drink. We made up for it though, both unemployed and living off the deployment money, we lived. Weekend after weekend we lived. Her efforts to save me were exponential as time went on and I drank more and more.

One raucous night we left the bar and I got in my car and she got in her truck to head home. I only teetered a little bit walking in the parking lot. Boyfriend was in the passenger seat and I was going to drive. Once Marie saw me in the driver's seat, she got out of her truck and stomped up to my window.

"What do you think you're doing?" she yelled at me. "Get out, you're not driving."

"But I have my GPS on!" I replied and pointed at the GPS stuck to my windshield for effect.

I didn't drive that night. She was my real-life guardian angel, only a lot angrier and wore more black and tighter jeans.

Once my unemployment money ran out in 2009, it was time to get a "real job." I put in applications for a year and a half with nothing. A Bachelor's in Social Work wasn't a guaranteed ticket to a job so at that point I was willing to take what I could get. Most of the places I applied to wanted experience in actual clinical work. Even the places I applied to volunteer at wouldn't call me back.

I spent most of the previous year unemployed, sleeping, and gaining weight. People always commented to me how awesome it would be to not have a job, they said they would have "so much time to do stuff", as they waved their hands in the air somehow signifying "stuff."

That's the thing about not working, when you don't have a purpose, something to wake you up every day, eating cool whip out of the can seems like the most exciting thing you'll do that day. I did a lot of stuff all right. I spent countless hours at my local video rental place, picking up questionable movies about drag queens and drank a lot. Seriously Bill Murray, WHAT WAS WRONG WITH THE NECK TIE SCENE, WHY WON'T YOU ANSWER ME ON TWITTER, AND WHY DID YOU ALWAYS SEEM TO HAVE A LEMON IN EVERY SCENE YOU WERE IN FOR TOOTSIE?!

Generally, I just spent a lot of time on the floor of my room, in my childhood home, living with mom, in the fetal position occasionally turning to my back to stare at the ceiling.

Magically, as my time and money were running out, the police department my mom worked at was hiring for a civilian position. I put in my application, but I had absolutely no hope I'd get the job. The interview was a favor to mom.

I made sure to wear a shirt and jacket that covered my tattoo on my collarbone. I researched the department the previous night, and thought about how to turn my weaknesses into strengths, because that is interviewers favorite question to ask. Oh, I don't know, Sharon, even though I generally hate doing work, I'll show up for the paycheck. I still haven't figured out how to turn inappropriate mannerisms in an office setting into a strength. The word fuck is my go-to reaction in most situations; I eat food off of the floor, use chewing tobacco, and hate real pants.

Once I arrived at the interview, I had to wait my turn so I sat out in the lobby, which smelled like pee. I have a question, our dear Lord and Savior, why is the scent of urine an overarching theme in my life? WHY?

I fidgeted in the chair, crossed my legs, and shook my foot. At one point, the big boss lady came out into the hall and said I looked nervous. "Well, no shit lady, my future earnings and general feelings about my self-worth depend on how this day goes, how am I supposed to look?" I guessed I was supposed to look confident or excited.

Absolutely not, I thought. "I am most definitely not a grownup yet, I can't feel confident in a grownup situation. I don't even know what a sump pump is, or is it sub pump, when do you learn the difference?" I didn't say any of that. I just shrugged and plastered a smile on my face trying to imply that whole, whadd'ya gonna' do, vibe.

Somehow, I pulled it off and I was offered the job. I think maybe when they asked how I would feel if any human 'fluids' got on me, I replied that it would be fine. I was told that part of the job was to fingerprint inmates at the jail. Apparently, there was a legitimate chance that human fluids could get on me during a workday. Oh sign me right the fuck up. I told them I'd already had human feces on me (Iraq ya'll), so, again, it'd be fine.

My first day of work, I got ready for my big outing and decided I needed to eat breakfast like an adult would do, so I pulled out a jar of peanut butter. This wasn't your kid's sweet and creamy peanut butter. It was some bright yellow, organic, and cinnamon flavored butter-of-the-peanut-concoction. It was neon yellow. What I wasn't aware of as I yanked the lid off was the oil in it had risen to the top and obviously I spilled it all over my shirt, making it look like I massaged my chest with mustard.

Very un-adult like, I went to my mom's room and…shut up, yes I was still living with her at the age of 25…I bawled and cried and told her what happened, but like the saint she was, she got up, got a rag and somehow scrubbed that shit out. I stood in the kitchen shirtless, tears still running down my cheeks as she worked her mom skills. Did I mention I would be making 20 bucks an hour at this job? Well, I was. I had no idea what to do with that much money. I knew it bought a lot of beer and Cosmopolitan magazines.

I made it on time that day and mostly every other day for the next seven years. The first year working there was hell. Eight hours at a computer was something I hadn't planned on in the adult version of myself. It seemed to take forever to catch onto things, but I was assured that's why the probation period was so long, there were a lot of things to learn, like how to calm a drunk person down as you tried to maneuver their hands and wrists in awkward positions as you fingerprinted them.

The fingerprinting aspect was the most interesting part of the job. I'm not proud to admit this, but seeing people at their least gracious times in life made me feel a little bit better about my grownup skills. Now, I have issues with our justice system as a whole, but when men slugged their wives and came into lockup drunk, I didn't have a lot of sympathy for their decisions in life. Many times, the wives would come into the police department the next day and I would take pictures of their bruises and scrapes. At lockup, I took those men's hands and recorded their misdeeds on my machine and I didn't feel bad about it, especially when their knuckles were cut up from meeting their beautiful wife's cheekbones.

It was always about the hands. I never recognized the faces from reoffenders, but I knew their hands. I often thought about how I'd held so many people's hands while working there. Even through my anger at some of the inmates, regardless of the charges against them, I tried to find their humanness in the act of touching them as I stood there in silence.

One night I processed a younger girl with drug charges. She was really sleepy and could barely stand up, but hey, she was nice enough. I took her hand in mine to get her prints on the machine. Jerkily, she pulled her hand away and started grabbing at my legs. She batted at them lightly, so I wasn't scared she was trying to hurt me. I stepped away from her with my hands out, in case she started to get really wiry. The confinement officers were located in a separate area from the fingerprinting room, but I decided not to call out for help.

"What are you doing hun'?" I asked.

She mumbled, "I, I dropped my cigarette."

"No, no you didn't," I said. "You're in jail, you don't have a cigarette right now."

A minute later, I was almost finished with her paperwork and she started pulling on a drawer of my computer printer. "What are you doing?" I whispered.

"I'm getting a drink out of the fridge," she whispered back.

"Nope again, that's not the fridge, that's a printer," I said.

Drugs are bad kids. In fact, let me say this again, adults...drugs are bad, and that includes recreational and prescribed painkillers.

I eventually got my own apartment a year after starting at the police department. For a few weeks, I sat on the floor to eat dinner and watched a lot of episodes of ladies that lived in a certain city and they had loads of sex. Am I talking about Sex and the City or the Golden Girls? You'll never know because I'll never tell. I watched the show on repeat because I didn't have cable. I consider it a glorious testament of my adulthood that I managed to get the DVD player hooked up to the television all by myself. I even got a futon so it could double as a couch and bed for guests, hey look at me all looking out for the future.

Naturally, the next step in my life was to get a dog. His name was Dozer and he was the love of my life. I only had three mini breakdowns over raising him. Good news is, he only sent me to the hospital once and he only had to go to the doggy hospital twice.

Um, did you guys know that puppies lose their baby teeth? I DIDN'T! I woke up one day and there was blood smeared on the wall and I was sure my puppy had been murdered during the night. I found him just sitting in the living room, looking cute like usual. Then I found a tooth on the floor. "Oh, well that's how that works," I thought.

Come on all you past adults, you have got to be better at raising us because there is no reason that information shouldn't have trickled down to me at some point in my life.

Another year later, I decided I was tired of following Dozer around waiting for him to poop. The apartment was nice, but it took him near forty minutes to deuce, all the while with me pleading for him to "Just goooo!" I then took the next step to being a boss in life, I bought a house. My number one requirement was that it had to have a fenced in back yard, you know, for the pooping.

Here's the problem with being an adult: No one ever sits you down and says how the dirty details of surviving should go. They're too busy teaching us pre-calculus. They say vague things like, "You'll understand one day," or "Just you wait, life's going to get hard, it's shitty and then you die." Well that's absolutely no help, and just fucking lazy.

So, to save you some headaches, here are some things you should know as a grown ass person. I make no guarantees as to the accuracy of any of these statements but here we are:

When you buy a house, there's this thing called a mortgage. The mortgage is a huge important thing that you promise to take care of, but a bank has to give you the right to take care of it, by giving you a piece of paper saying they'll take care of it. The bank will need to know a lot of things about you and make educated punches in the dark that you can handle it. The bank eventually says, yes, yes we'll let you burden yourself with crushing debt. Then, you pay the bank on a monthly basis and you'll most likely have a longer relationship with that bank than you will most friends. The banks will tell you that you can afford to get a really, really big mortgage and they'll say it'll be fine. That's a lie. Go ahead, take the number they give you, and reduce that by about $50,000. That should be the size of mortgage you get, you know, if you like to eat food while under shelter.

When you move into this house, you will have to call the water, gas, electric companies, and the trash place so you can legally get shit done while in that house. Your washer and dryer will be either gas or electric, how you figure that out without someone telling you, I'm not sure, you'll have to figure it out yourself. Marie installed my washer and dryer because Boyfriend was in Iraq at the time I moved in. Marie literally knew everything about everything, find you a Marie.

Here's a fun one: Bills have a due date, but then they have this magical date called the "past due" date. You will have to Tetris your finances to not pay after the "past due" date, but very rarely do you have to pay it on the legit due date. Automatic bill payments are oh so convenient, but I can't make my mortgage come out of my account automatically because sometimes I must wait until there's money actually in there, then I pay it over the phone. Side note, the thing with talking to people on the phone as an adult is, you should act like a kid. You should sound really sorry that you're late and thank them a lot when they graciously tell you they won't charge you the late fee this time.

Garbage disposals are shit.

When I lived in the apartment, whenever the disposal quit working, I'd just call a number, some guy would fix it while I was gone and then I'd see a pile of chicken bones on the counter that I swore I never put in there in the first place.

Now, the garbage disposal in my sink at home doesn't work. That basically means that side of the sink doesn't work, so I just use the other side. Fixed.

As an adult, there's no one there to tell you to sweep and mop the floors. This means, it mostly only gets done when you suddenly have a second dog and you think you own a third one because the hair blowing around has formed into another, third being. At some point though, you morph into a cleaning machine and you're scrubbing your toilet with a beer in your hand.

By far, one of the worst things I learned as an adult was that for the rest of my life, I would have to buy things at the store I don't want to buy. As a kid and tween, I saved up for makeup, cd's, or shirts that mom would never buy me. But oh no, as an adult, you will have to buy toilet paper, dish soap, laundry soap, toothpaste, sheets, tampons, mouse traps, and all kinds of shit that kills your heart a little every time you do it. But, if you're thrifty, you can get a membership at Costco, and then buy it all, once a year. This is slightly less painful. A HUNDRED COUNT TAMPON BOXES PEOPLE!!! A HUNDRED!

You must, must maintain your vehicle. Now, I could easily (not really easily) change my own oil, but that's not going to happen. I'm much more comfortable paying someone else to do things I don't want to and in the long run I think it's going to keep years tacked onto my life.

Here's the fun part of being an adult though.

You can have sex whenever you want. I know right, it's crazy. So, then why are all these grownups out and about, walking around, doing you know, other stuff than sex? I mean you have your own place, with your own bedroom that you don't have to keep the door open when you go in it with a boy. Hell, you have the entire rest of the house to yourself. You're free to do whatever you want; besides cook meth, meth is bad.

Did you know it's perfectly acceptable to have sex in your basement, next to the weight bench? Well, you should know that. You can even do it by yourself there, you don't even need another person present, and no one's going to burst into the bathroom asking for the tweezers when you're doing the sex stuff to yourself.

As a teenager, sex took up a huge portion of my thoughts. All thoughts went into trying to figure out when I could do it again. It consumed my squishy body day and night. So, it's curious to me that once I grew up, there was so much less sex in my life than I thought there would be.

I think the problem is, as a kid, my life was all about me. The dishes, the laundry, the cleaning, it was all mom's responsibility and I only helped when she screamed at me to. My literal job was to eat, sleep, and do homework. That left a lot of mental space to think about the sexy time. I fused into my own brain when fantasizing as a teenager, I could spend twenty minutes thinking of how I'd take my shirt off in front of a guy. Now, I just fantasize about someone else unloading the dishwasher, because I hate that shit.

When Boyfriend came back from Iraq and we'd lived together for a while, we began to lag in the doing it tally marks. I'd fall into bed after work and all the other things I didn't want to do that day were still piled up. I spotted dust balls leading to my bed and I saw spider webs on the ceiling. Once in bed, I would roll over and he would start the groping, but then I would look over his shoulder at his sweater and pants lying on top of the bedroom dresser. If I rolled over to the other side, I saw the empty water glasses (those were from me) sitting on the other bedside table and it would force me to think about what a slob I was. It all did nothing to get my juices flowing. Eww, that was gross sounding and I will never say it again.

I didn't know what the fix was to any of this though and I still don't. I just liked to bitch about it and nag him, because you know, the no sex thing makes Laura grumpy.

Back to the bad stuff, because from what I can see, there's more bad stuff than good once you hit 22. As an adult, you will also have to buy stuff for other people that you don't want to buy. Holidays, birthdays, engagements, house warming parties, cheer up presents, retirement presents, it never ends. This is why I'm still paying off my college loans, not my drinking problem.

I don't mind this part so much. One day, I hope to have an extravaganza day where I have all twenty lifelong parties at once. At this rate, it should happen in the year 2030. You will also never get as many presents as you give, sorry to break it to you kids, but that's just a fact of life. Fancy stores that sell decorations AND spinach will suck thousands of dollars' worth of last minute gift ideas from you, year after year, and you better either get used to it, or get better at planning ahead and buying things before the day of a party.

No one is there to tell you to eat your vegetables either, so you better figure out a way to make them delicious. Otherwise, you're not going to force yourself to eat them. Cocoa powder on cauliflower is a Godsend.

No one is going to tell you to get off the couch and stop watching another movie with more drag queens for the thousandth time. That's the fun part though, you get to decide when you're going to go out and play until the streetlights go off, and you still don't have to go home even after they do.

No one is going to ask you what you want to do when you grow up anymore, so you should probably figure it out at some point prior to getting off your parents' insurance. Note here: Planned Parenthood is spectacular when it comes to other things not including abortions (I can't attest to that procedure since I've always used Plan B so things never got that hairy). Hobo is in fact an option; but if you like baths, I don't suggest this route.

You will adore someone who isn't perfect, and sometimes crying will feel better than laughing, and laughing will be harder than crying, but it's worth it if you can manage.

One day though, you'll walk the maze that is the Land of Couches and grossly expensive cloth napkins, and you'll see a wooden tray that you just must have. At some point, you'll stop pining after cute clothes, and you'll look for things to decorate your house with. This is the first sign that you're a grownup, door hooks are your obsession, and caddies, caddies for makeup, for hair brushes, for kitchen counter thingies you have no idea where else to put. YOU WILL PURCHASE EVERY LAST SINGLE CADDY THAT EXISTS. And one day your life will be perfect, and stored. I'm lying here, it will never be perfect, but that's ok.

Here's one thing I've never stopped doing as an adult. I call my mom. Despite all the coping mechanisms I've come up with in my lifetime to handle stress or bad situations, I still call my mom. My first pull is always to pick up the phone and wail into it the second she says hello. She will tell me to breathe, because I've forgotten how, and I will breathe and I will live. Sometimes she even tells me things about escrow accounts that I pretend to understand.

I remember the exact day mom Spartan kicked me into self-awareness and adulthood. I was six-years-old and riding in the car with her. My super favorite jam of the decade was playing on the radio. Pump Up the Jam blared over her Toyota speakers. I was buckled in, but my restraints couldn't hold me down and I wiggled and pumped up my own jam, dancing in my seat. Much arm flailing ensued because duh, that's how you pump.

Mom looked over at me and said, "You know Laura, the people in other cars can see you."

It was like she had slapped me. I furrowed my brow and transitioned into slow motion as I sat back in my seat, ending my dance in a lifeless and still slump. Mom had instantly blown up my concept of reality in that moment. I dropped out of the impression that I was the universe and I was in it alone. As a kid, I thought I was simply alive to enjoy myself, completely independent of anyone else's thoughts or opinions. I had to learn some day I guess. I realized eventually, I could unlearn some adult things though. When I drive now, as an adult who updates her car and house insurance yearly, as an adult who understands the importance of a Health and Savings Account, I belt out songs to my hearts' content and I wriggle in my seat, regardless if anyone is looking or not.

# Not the Worst Thing That's Ever Happened

In college, I frequented bars so often that not only did I know the bartenders' names, but I also knew their last names along with their favorite cousin's middle name and I had crushes on every single one of them. I'd sometimes take the University bus to downtown Bloomington, hit the first bar on the corner and made my way around the loop to head home. That's what I thought I was supposed to be doing, besides getting a degree. For the most part, it didn't get me into a ton of trouble, the legal kind anyways.

The best thing about not having a car while in college was the added cardio sessions of sporadic drunken sprints down Kirkwood and the near impossibility of getting a DUI.

But once I left college, things became a little trickier. Bars weren't just around the corner anymore and there wasn't a drunk-bus to shuttle drunk-Laura back home. Remember, this was a time before Uber. Since graduating and moving into an honest to God house with a mortgage, I made it a hobby to stay at home when I drank. This was much more cost effective and no one minded when my underwear came off and I had my bouts of hopping spells.

For some reason when I became inebriated, I had the urge to get everywhere by hopping up and down to various locations. That was usually when friends cut me off from booze, if I happened to be out and about in town. But at home, I could bounce to my heart's content.

One rare night friends convinced me to go over to their house for a random, "It's a Saturday" party, which doesn't happen very often once you reach the age of 25 and have friends with children and responsibilities that go beyond putting clothes in the dryer.

I walked into the house and there were four people standing around in a semi-dark kitchen. As soon as everyone noticed I was there, someone chucked keys at my face, saying,

"We are going out and you are driving."

"Ok drunk person, but I don't drive other people's cars," I said, throwing the keys back at the person.

Shortly after, I stuffed five people into my Toyota Corolla and headed out. The bar itself wasn't that bad really…if you like country bars that play soft rock songs that talk about infidelity and eyes of otherworldly beings.

I started off slow, milking one beer until someone noticed I was a bit behind. Boyfriend was working late and I didn't want to be shitfaced when he got there, just to prove a point, the point that I don't get shitfaced when you're not around "point".

Someone noticed I had the same beer from an hour ago, what with the soggy label half torn off, and me no closer to periodically groping strangers because I wasn't even buzzed yet.

Then a curious thing happened, the same thing that happens once every three seconds in America, and the same thing that causes thousands of unwanted pregnancies, tattoos, and threesomes in a year.

Someone yelled, "Shot, shot, shot, shot, shot, shot."

At some point, I ended up sitting at the bar next to some stranger talking about 90's TV shows, and the little tidbit I'd heard about a new Not Adults Possibly Extraterrestrial Reptiles with Shells movie being remade, and how absurd it was that they were taking the 'mutant' out of the title supposedly. All of this took place as I attempted to stuff potato skins into my mouth, only to succeed in getting sour cream all over my cheeks. That's possibly a good look in porn movies, but for God's sake, not in public next to strange men.

"It's a travesty I tell ya', A FUCKING TRAJECTORY!" I said to the man.

"I know right," he said. "I heard they're aliens now."

Boyfriend had shown up by then, but he usually mingled separate from me so it took him a bit to get around to visiting with me. Eventually he saw me lay my head on the bar, which is our cue, it's time to take Laura home.

This night, he didn't take me home. This night, I insisted I was fine to drive, I wanted to take my own car, and he could follow behind me. My slurred words should never be trusted though, because remember, I'm the same person who once told a friend I was ok to drive because I had my GPS on. Because the GPS never steers you wrong.

The bar was a good 20 to 30 minutes away from my house and I thought I was actually doing fine after almost making it home. Sure, I hit the occasional curb, but that happens when I'm stone sober. I had less than five minutes before I'd be home. The plan was, I'd go inside, pee about

16 times, leave my pants in the bathroom where I always kick them off, and climb into bed.

That's when I looked in the rearview mirror and saw silly little blue and red lights.

I'd later find out Boyfriend had called me over and over on my cell phone. He had attempted to pull me over numerous times by pulling next to me and yelling out his window. All I heard though was my car radio. I was far too busy, singing along with pop sensation what's her face that sang about her sexuality being fluid. I belted and swore I was a fucking firework, and I was sure damn well going to let it burst, so I never noticed Boyfriend trying to flag me down.

It took me a minute to realize the lights were definitely not flashing to let me know they were going to pass me on their way to some crazy drug bust or pineapple stuck up in a tree. They were for me.

Then, Officer Griffin (names have been changed to protect the innocent) walked up to my window, shining his flashlight on me. I instantly recognized him, you know because I worked at the POLICE DEPARTMENT.

"Heeeey, old buddy old pal," I'm sure I said, but this whole part is a little blurry. I ended up blowing a blood alcohol level of .17, so I can't be held accountable for the following details I recall from this point on.

The officer dropped his head a little in a "oh, god not you, anyone but you" sort of way. I don't mean to toot my own horn here or anything, but I think I was a likeable person around the office. I photo copied and typed up reports like a motherfucker and I had done some administration work for this detective on a number of occasions. Like, we were on a weekly email basis type of working relationship.

I never blamed him though. After the arrest, a lot of people at work said it was unbelievable that he arrested me. I can say I owe a part of my new life to him because he arrested me. Yeah, I was only five minutes from my house, but within that five minutes, there could have been a family traveling home from visiting with their sick elderly grandparents, there could have been someone walking home from the bars like a responsible person, and I could have plowed into them. Because I was pulled over and stopped, worse things didn't happen than me committing a misdemeanor and having to face the disgusting level my drinking had come to. Because of that arrest, I went to alcohol classes and continued seeing a therapist at the VA. Though I continued to drink, it was no longer something I did to pass the time and get away from what I looked at in the mirror. Because Griffin didn't cut me a break like everyone thought he should have, I kind of sort of got my shit together.

I could have been mad that someone I knew arrested me, but I never was. I was thankful. We are all responsible, in huge proportions for the things that happen to us. I was no less accountable for getting in my car and deciding I didn't give a shit if I killed someone or not. Just because I worked with the officer at the police department, it made me no less guilty of committing a crime.

Boyfriend had no other choice but to continue driving home, where he then called my mom to tell her I'd been arrested.

In a strange way, I kind of resent that I wasn't handcuffed. Now, my memory can't be relied upon and he very well could have handcuffed me, but I don't think he did. I mean really, if you're going to do anything, you should go balls out. I also sometimes regret I didn't at least play like a limp dead girl when I was arrested, and made them carry me into the holding cell like a little princess on her way to a tower.

Griffin opened his squad car door for me to get into. I looked inside and immediately wanted to turn and run. The police vehicle had a clear plastic partition between the front and back of the interior of the car, and in the back seat was a small metal stool of a seat.

"Holy fuck, it's the Death Proof car", which I didn't say out loud but I thought it.

Now if you haven't seen Death Proof, I'll enlighten you. It basically starts out with a group of pot smoking, trash talking cool girls I know I'd be best friends with in real life, if only I looked good in shorts and smoked pot.

These girls go out partying and end up at a bar. One of the girls keeps seeing an old muscle car creeping by as they go from bar to bar. Stuntman Mike, played by Kurt Russell, is stalking them. In one particularly gruesome scene, Kurt Russell, who wears an eye patch, offers to take a random girl home in his "stunt car". She's a little weirded out at first because the passenger seat is separated by a glass looking barrier (Just like the vehicle I was about to get into) and there was no seat belt for the passenger. She gets in anyways, because you know, women rely on the kindness of strangers, and he inevitably bludgeons her to death by repeatedly slamming on his breaks and then gas, flinging her back and forth in her seat against the shatter proof partition.

I froze, looking inside the car.

"Stuntman Mike, oh please no, Stuntman Mike," I whispered to myself as I got into the car. "I'm so totally going to be murdered, where's the seatbelt, there's no seatbelt," I rambled on. "I don't want to get my teeth knocked out, that's the absolute worst thing that could happen in life, I love corn on the cob, and knocked out teeth will just not work with a cob eating kind of lifestyle. Oh my God, I have glasses on, they're totally going to crack and then glass shards are going to be in my eyeballs."

The problem was, Griffin got into the driver's seat and I felt like everything was going all wrong. "You can't be the one to murder me, you only have a lazy eye (which he totally did), not an eye patch, it's all wrong." It was ok if Kurt Russell killed me because he was hot in an old man crying sort of way (Stuntman Mike cries like a baby seal at the end of the movie because the female hero's start whooping his ass).

"Where the fuck are you Kurt Russell … Quentin… anyone?"

"What?" asked Griffin.

I did not die that night. I lived, and possibly so did someone else because I was arrested. I'd call that a good night.

# Why is There a Toothbrush in the Bushes

I reminisce more about seemingly unimportant things than epic life events. I don't often think about my college years or my first deployment. Instead, I think about situations I will never understand or fully know. Life isn't about the big moments though, so I've found it important to see the small ones.

I wonder about long gone lollipop sticks.

Smoke breaks took up a lot of my little moments when I worked at the police department. One afternoon, I sat outside on a bench and noticed a lollipop stick on the ground. Slightly bent, the little white twig had only a small pink crumble left on it. Why would someone just throw it on the ground, I wondered. There was a trash can nearby. I disregarded the stick and went back inside. The next day the lollipop stick was sitting on top of the bench, instead of on the ground. Now, who would pick it up off the ground and put it on the bench? Maybe a squirrel did it, I thought. I would take drags on my cigarette and stare at the stick on the bench. I wanted to know, who was eating a lollipop outside a police station, maybe a detective trying to quit smoking. Every day I would find it. The tightly rolled white paper stem got blacker each day with dirt, as it continued to sit there for a good month straight. Sometimes the stick would be in a slightly different place on the bench. I couldn't bring myself to throw it away. Even the ants didn't want it anymore.

Finally, I went out to smoke one day and the lollipop stick was gone. I remember feeling quite sad. Now what would I look at while I killed myself just a little bit, one break at a time.

Walking my dogs was another daily life practice for me. Things were usually calm on walks with Dozer and Junior. Obviously, they can't talk to me, they're dogs. It's a quiet time that can bring a lot of internal chaos, or silence, depending on the day. I've found that if I just pay attention to my surroundings, I can keep the monsters at bay. My favorite thing to keep me occupied, while they sniffed and lollygagged, was to look at things people had thrown onto the roads and sidewalks. People are disgusting by the way.

I knew every piece of trash left on the ground to decay had a story and it killed me sometimes that I didn't know what that story was, so I tried to make things up.

The entire tin of lasagna, just right in the middle of the sidewalk was probably from a lovers' spat. Vito probably spent the night playing the accordion to some other Bella, and he thought he'd be slick by bringing home a pan of lasagna, you know, so Vikki didn't have to cook that night. Well, Vikki probably wasn't having any of that so she slapped the pan out of Vito's hand, but he hugged her anyways and they played hide the cannoli to make it all better that night. Mmm, cannoli.

The whole chicken leg in an alley was probably leftovers that ninja raccoons found in the trash, but their epic battle ended up in both of them being mortally wounded, leaving the chicken leg alone. I then had to shove my hand down Dozer's throat as he tried to swallow it in one go.

There's the same stuff most of the time; empty shooter bottles of alcohol that someone was too ashamed to drink in front of anyone else. There were a lot of used condoms that I don't even want to imagine where they came from. There were empty Dorito bags that couldn't have possibly filled anyone up. The piles of boxes and mattresses that sat in front of dark houses made me feel the worst. There were usually kids' toys and clothes in the mix and I wonder where they moved to, that they couldn't take the stuff with them.

One day, I saw something in my neighbor's hedge bushes that I just couldn't come up with a credible and absolute story for.

The walk was almost over, as I would just have to pass the bushes, make my way to the alley on the left, into the garage, through to the backyard, and into my house. I stopped in front of the bushes because I saw something white and orange caught in the branches. It was a toothbrush, an adult's toothbrush. There were various other wrappers and trash on the ground around the bright green and waxy looking bush, but the toothbrush just sat there, right on top. There was a window right next to the bush.

Ok, so maybe the bushes were the neighbor's trashcan. They just chucked things out of the window. But, I mean, their bathroom is probably upstairs like mine is, so they'd have to carry the toothbrush all the way downstairs to throw it out of the window. Don't these people have bathroom trash bins? Then I thought maybe one of the kids in the house, I never did see an adult from those neighbors, was like, "fuck nah, ain't going to be no teeth brushing today, especially with this big ass toothbrush that hurts my baby gums," and got rid of the awful toothbrush of torture so their ghost mom wouldn't find it.

I left it at that, irritated that there was a toothbrush in the bushes, and went inside. I thought about it for the rest of my day.

The next day, I was almost home again with the dogs when I stopped at the street right before my house. There was a bearded guy on an old timey bicycle turning onto my road so I waited for him to pass.

He was the epitome of hipster. He was wearing corduroy pants with his man satchel and had a tousled brown man-bun sitting all cute on top of his head. He probably had a scarf on and his name was most likely Holden. We locked eyes as he turned the corner. He looked at me, brought a coffee mug up to his lips and took a sip of what I assumed was coffee. This wasn't a gas station-I'm-on-the-move-got-things-to-do type of coffee Styrofoam cup. It was a legit coffee cup. He merrily pedaled down the street and I continued to stand on the corner curb, brow furrowed, as he flew out of sight.

I stomped my foot and watched him fade into a tiny dot of pompousness. Who the hell drinks hot coffee while riding their bike? I saw the steam.

I was jealous of his coolness. I can't effectively carry my coffee cup from the kitchen to the dining room without sloshing some of it out. The instant I lift the mug from the counter, I instantaneously forget I have liquid in a cup in my hand. Since I forget the key component to beverage transporting without a lid, I wildly swing my arm around, while looking forward, dribbling along the hallway. I might as well do jumping jacks while holding it.

Who did this asshole think he was, sipping on what was most likely a slow drip coffee concoction aged in a cheese barrel, with a splash of vegan breast milk and dash of saffron and patchouli oil…ON A BIKE?!!!

"AhhhhhHAAA!" I screamed and pointed in his direction, still holding on to the dogs' leashes. "You put the toothbrush in bushes didn't you, you, you, Jonas stepbrother twice removed you!" I yelled after him. "But why did you DO IT?"

I went home and promptly used the sink hose to fill up my coffee pot, and I put on some grocery store coffee to brew.

# Running Nowhere

As much as I'm awed by the big magical events in my life, I find I'm more attracted to the little "off" things that find their way into the periphery of my life. Maybe it's because I'm free to stare at the ground or sky, or in whichever direction the thunder's coming from. I have this underlying belief that I don't have all the time in the world to notice things, so I grasp the small things as fiercely as I can.

Another very NOT unique thing that was always important to me was traveling. Over my 33 years, I've tried to do as much of it as my bank account has allowed. Courtesy of the Army, I was able to go on adventures to Iraq and Afghanistan for deployments. I've traveled to Costa Rica, Puerto Rico, Alaska, and Canada. Not a long list, I know, but those places made me feel insignificant.

This makes me sound like a pretentious shit, I get it, I can hear you saying, "Ooo, another Millenial traveler who thinks she's a special crystalized snowflake making these amazing observations." I was grateful to be able to see the things I had. I went to Costa Rica in high school and never felt like I deserved something less than I did that trip. My parents somehow made it happen, and who knows what credit card was maxed out for it.

I thought I'd find all the things that make this odd trip of life worth it by wandering the Denali trails in Alaska. I traveled only nine miles into the thick of it and I know I didn't touch on even a drop of what was there. In the span of a week, I saw the season change. The trees trumpeted oranges and yellows, colors that didn't even show up in my dreams, they were that beautiful. The mountains looked like living breathing monsters that were simply taking naps.

I felt things more intimately when I zoomed into the small details of the that trip and found delight in the things I could take mental snapshots of and only guess at what they could mean. The bear poop on the trail alluded to a dangerous excitement that the actual hiking didn't bring. It was a small pile, deep purple with berries in it that looked quite pretty, like wine. I never saw a bear, but there was the chance, and that was exciting.

While hiking one day, Boyfriend's step-mom, Michelle, was having some issues getting up and down hills. She had been so proud of the special hiking shoes she'd gotten from Goodwill's online store. She said they would help her navigate the treacherous Tundra. I didn't really know what the Tundra was exactly, but I figured it was the soft, wet ground within the forests of Alaska.

"Wait a minute, you're telling me Goodwill has a website?" I asked, looking at the purple spiky shoes as she adjusted and readjusted the Velcro straps on them.

"Yeah, I got them for like eight bucks," said Michelle.

As the day wore on she became more frustrated. She said she needed to take a pee break, so she cut into the trees, off of the trail. Muffled by the pine trees, I heard the sound of a yelp coming from Michelle. We rushed into the forest, sure at least a goat or something was attacking her. There, splayed out in the bushes, her face red in embarrassment, with her short hair plastered to her face with sweat, she was panting. She wasn't hurt, but she had fallen down.

"I got the tundra in my pants!" Michelle yelled in her Southern accent, rolling around in the moss. Finally, she sat up and chucked the shoes off and said she wasn't going to wear them anymore.

Boyfriend knelt to help her and started laughing even harder than he already was. He held one of the shoes in his hand and shook his head.

Boyfriend said, "Michelle, these…these aren't hiking shoes. They're bicycling shoes, see these straps here, they're supposed to hook to the bike pedals."

"Well how the hell was I supposed to know that?" Michelle asked.

It struck me as funny because I'm sure whoever got rid of those shoes had no idea that someone would buy them, fully intending to hike the Denali Trail wearing them.

I'm sure I bitched and moaned more than I remember during the hike because I could never quite keep up with Boyfriend in any physical displays. I basically have the agility of a giraffe on a tightrope when it comes to climbing on rocks and mountains. I'm not scared of heights at all, that's not the problem, I'm scared of sliding down rock faces and shredding my face skin off and breaking an ankle by falling off a five-centimeter tall rock.

In the beginning of the hike, I was scared. I feared the openness and falling into a crevice where no one could reach me.

Towards the end though, I focused on each step. The trail turned into a level rock staircase, which only slightly twisted and turned. I looked around and I was surrounded by gray trees, their dressings laid at their feet in layers of brown and red dead leaves. Beneath the leaves, the emerald green moss hugged the rocks on the trail in a slippery embrace.

"I'm going to run up ahead," I told Boyfriend.

I took off and kept a good mile in front of the rest of the group. I count that run, as only one of two, in my entire life that didn't hurt. It's weird, I don't remember if I had my headphones in or not, which I normally can't run without. When I run, it's an ordeal. I run because, if I don't, I'd basically be an overweight Hobbit, with smaller, less hairy feet. Being overweight isn't in and of itself a bad thing, I just haven't come to a place where I'm ok with not fitting into the clothes I already have.

I usually think about how much my thighs rub together, or how much my boobs hurt because they're bouncing. I think about how heavy my arms feel because I can't figure out the right angle to hold them. My lungs burned abnormally because I was a smoker. My nose ran, and my butt cheeks were numb from the shaking. I usually pull at all my clothes, my shorts ride up, my shirts fall over my bum, making it look fatter than it is and I just can't have that. There's usually one bone, out of the oh I don't know, hundred or so, in my foot that I'm sure is broken because it aches, it aches along with the stitch in my right rib cage. I can never breathe in enough air and I almost pee myself ninety percent of the time from the effort.

This run though, it was the reason runners insist on putting one foot in front of the other day after day, and that run became that which I thought wasn't possible, that run was joyful.

It was like there was a ukulele in the background, edging me on with its inherently cheerful sound. (Side note, to whomever plans my funeral…there better be a ukulele playing next to my casket, seriously, make that shit happen).

There was no huffing or puffing. I let air in and out like it was natural or something. My arms swung gracefully, I leaped over rocks, and down the chiseled stairs. At that moment, it felt like I could have run forever and my legs weren't tired.

I'm not sure why the run felt the way it did. Maybe it was because I wasn't going for time, I wasn't going for miles, I wasn't going just until I reached my house. I just went. I had no idea when the trail would end. I can't say I even looked out into the woods. I looked at the ground directly ahead and my own feet, my own marvelous, wonderful feet, in an old black and muddy pair of Nike's carrying me.

You might say, well yeah, you were in Alaska, who wouldn't have an awesome run there, it's so beautiful and there's many things to look at to take your mind off of the pain. FUCKING MOUNTAIN AIR, THAT'S WHAT THAT THERE IS, they might say.

To that I say, not so.

The Alaska run was great, but I had the absolute best run of my life while in boot camp in the Army.

A few weeks into basic training, we had a new addition to the company. The female recruit, Thompson, we'll call her, had been passed on from other units who didn't want her because she had quit. She refused to train. She wouldn't listen to the Drill Sergeants and she just screamed back at them. She wanted to go home, she said. Unfortunately, she had signed a contract with the U.S. Government. The girl had lady balls though.

One awful day, the drill sergeants told us to go run around the track, but she wouldn't do it. They told us, one way or another we better move her around that track within the next two minutes or we'd pay. That meant, if we didn't accomplish the mission, we'd be rolling around in the tire pit for a few hours. The tire pit was this lovely play area outside filled with shredded pieces of tire. I'm convinced if you took a sample from any section of it, it would test positive for vomit, and tears.

A group of other female Soldiers surrounded her and started pulling her along. She swung and we were told we had the right to defend ourselves. I never laid hands on her, but I know I was part of the cloud that pushed her around that track. I will never know what she felt that day, being forced to do something she didn't want to. Her body was not her own.

After that day, she started falling in with the training.

She was the loudest Private in the Company. Everything became, "Yes Drill Sergeant."

After a couple weeks of being the most motivated Soldier in the unit, Thompson could go on pass for church on Sunday.

She never came back after services.

Satan Drill Sergeant himself was screaming in the barracks that she had to be found and a group was taken to go look for her, along with the other Drill Sergeants. Meanwhile, the rest of us had no baby sitter so we were all put to the running track once more. We were told to run laps while the search took place off base. We had no idea how long or far we were supposed to run. We were left alone while the Drill Sergeants made phone calls inside.

I was so angry. I cursed Thompson as I stepped out onto the track to begin running. The first three laps, my mind took hold and all I could think of was how it wasn't fair. I fought it for the first forty minutes. Why should I be punished? I'd done everything right, I did what I was told when I was told. I didn't want to be there, I wanted to go home, and drink and laugh and play. With tears running down my face, I pumped my arms in a fit as I ran.

For me, the worst part of being a female in the Army is, when I get mad, I cry. I do the very thing everyone whispers girls are going to do when they're upset. I hate this about myself. I started calling myself a pussy and probably shrieked in my madness. I'm pretty sure I shouted a "fuck you" here or there at random people as I passed them on the track as they walked. Either way, right or wrong, we were supposed to be running and they didn't give a shit what was happening. They just strolled around the track like this was normal. I clopped along, feeling broken and heavy as a dump truck.

"Just run, Laura," I heard.

No one said it. I just heard it.

The tears stopped coming and the wind dried up what was already there. The sun kept ducking behind clouds and I could hear crows circling overhead and see the rust colored track underfoot. Eventually a smile spread across my face and I kept running as my tears turned to sweat.

"Down by the river..." I heard a group singing off in the distance as other Soldiers marched back from dinner and I kept running. I started to even pass Privates that were normally faster than me. It could have been an hour later, it could have been three, I don't know, but we were corralled inside and put to bed.

I was sorry to stop.

I don't know if they ever found Thompson, a mystery I'm fine with not knowing. I do know I slept like I was at home that night. I drifted off to sleep on my top bunk under the scratchy, green wool blanket, courtesy of the United States Army.

# Nano and the Brain

I have a complete and utter lack of understanding why I don't ever want to go to bed. It's not that I'm not tired, I'm always tired, it's just who I am as a person, tired. It's also not a fear of missing out on anything, because God knows even when I'm awake, I'm solid in the opinion that I'm the most exciting thing going on at any given time and I know if I'm asleep there's legitimately nothing that I will miss. When I say I'm exciting, I mean taking baths and watching awful horror movies easily entertain me. The fact is, I have the inability to put myself to bed at a decent hour.

I don't get it, sleep is my favorite thing, but only once I'm already doing it. It's the falling to sleep that really trips me up. I've tried concocting a bedtime ritual to put myself in the mood. It washes the skin, it puts the cream on the face, it reads the books and shuts off the TV, it does nightly meditations and breathes deeply. Granted, all these things start at a time way past what's considered normal. I usually start my nighttime ritual at about 2am.

I can credit those good old little pink allergy pills as the only thing that is a tried and true first step to drugging me just enough to lay down. I've halfheartedly tried to get doctors to give me Ambien. Word on the street is that after you take it, you're supposed to immediately go to bed because that's how sleep medications are supposed to work. You take Ambien, lay down, and boom, off to dreaming about having a jet ski. The problem is, I wouldn't go straight to bed, and no one needs to see Laura on the morning news, singing Mariah Carey songs into a rolling pin microphone, on top of a roof while I'm wearing a romper, 'cause THAT'S what would happen if I took Ambien. I'd wait around to purposely hallucinate instead of going to bed. I've seen myself in a romper…I don't suggest anyone else see it.

Oftentimes, Benadryl is not enough, and I need more to do the trick. By that time, I'm contemplating buying the bottles of liquid medicine and calling it a night. I know I'm not unique in that my brain never shuts up when I tell it to. Another unfortunate thing about me, is if I don't get 13 hours of shuteye, I will be a horrible person and fantasize the entire next day about going to bed. Sometimes I'll take naps on the toilet. But there She is, my Brain telling me to lie in bed watching Internet videos four hours before I'm supposed to wake up. I have all these empty notebooks stacked everywhere, so I need to watch a video about what to do with them. Why is that a thing? Why must I keep dozens of journals, notepads, notebooks, agendas and other stationary items hoarded? I absolutely know I'm not the only one who does this, simply because there's thousands of articles and hundreds of videos that tell you what to do with those blank pages. Hang on, I'm going to go look up what kind of disorder that implies.

I've also used online videos to help put me to sleep. Autonomous Sensory Meridian Response videos have been a miracle in helping.

If you haven't watched ASMR videos, boy oh boy do I have a treat for you. Initially I found such success with the clips online, that I recommended them to other people I knew who couldn't sleep, but the conversation never really went well.

"So, ASMR is that weird tingly feeling you get when you're watching someone do something or talk about something," I told some random person within the first ten minutes of meeting them.

"What do you mean, 'do something', what do they do, what do they talk about, I'm confused," the stranger asked.

I'd have my reply ready, "Ok, so do you remember in school there would always be a teacher, that when they talked and moved their hands, the sound of their voice put you in a numbing lull, and you got tingles and you just kind of zoned into them and felt really relaxed?"

"Oh, you mean they were boring so you fell asleep?" they asked.

"No, not like that at all…ok, it's also like when someone plays with your hair, it feels really good."

"How can someone play with your hair if they're in a video?" they asked.

I harrumphed and tried to figure out a better way to explain it. "The people in the videos, they talk into the camera, and my favorite videos to watch are when the people in them pretend to do your makeup, they get really close to the camera and use makeup brushes to act like they're putting eye shadow or blush on your face, and they make these mouth sounds, like all spitty and it's just really calming…if that makes sense. Oh and miniature cooking, those ones are good too."

The stranger inevitably asked, "What the fuck are you talking about, miniature cooking?"

To try to explain it, I looked up the actual definition of ASMR, and made the person stare at it to see if they knew what I meant. This is what they read:

Autonomous Sensory Meridian Response (ASMR) is a term for a perceptual phenomenon, which is explained as a distinct, pleasurable tingling sensation in the head, scalp, back, and other regions of the body in response to visual, auditory, tactile, olfactory, or cognitive stimuli.

Then they stared at me with a scowl and said, "We're done here," and then The Sound of Silence song started playing as they turned their back on me.

But seriously, just look up ASMR videos, and you can thank me later.

On any given night, I can watch the videos and it's like having a real-life person read me a bedtime story, or someone in the video will role-play as a "caring friend" and they ask me about my day and pretend they care. There are so many categories of ASMR videos that it's sorta' scary how some of them pan out. I also get kind of weirded out about how stoked I get about watching someone unwrap bars of soap. That's literally all they do, they do nothing but unwrap packages of soap and it is magical and cozy sounding, and the crinkly plastic sounds delicious to my ears.

Things get rough though when I don't have Internet or I've lost my phone in the refrigerator for the night.

This leads to me staring at the wall while I lay in bed. The blanket hurts my skin, my hip is sore from pressing into the mattress, my throat is dry, the sound of my own breathing is annoying, my legs are hot, but my arms are cold. I do that thing where just as I'm drifting off into Justin Long's arms – I fart which causes me to jolt and wake completely the fuck back up. The pillow hurts my hair, my sweatshirt is laying in a weird way so that I can feel it, and I have a wedgie. I realize I could alleviate some of my sleep issues by sleeping naked, but that's my business, don't go doling out advice here, this is my book Ann Landers.

Some people ponder life's huge mysteries while trying to fall asleep, while I take a more distinct route of worrying about my daily problems or incredibly random things that I have no business wondering about. It's a tug of war with my young adult Brain and I know it's not a phenomenon only I face, but it feels like I'm the only one in the world who argues with myself after I've eaten a Slim Jim and possibly moldy chocolate while simultaneously sitting on the toilet at 3am. I consider Afghanistan the only acceptable place to eat while sitting on the toilet.

Here's how the conversation with my Brain usually goes at night. They happened a lot in Afghanistan because the Internet goes out a lot there so I couldn't watch my videos. I know, I had it so rough.

Me: "Alright, let's get to bed now Brain, hush, it's sleepy time."

Brain: Squints it's wrinkles at me, "Um, no, no I don't think so, you have absolutely no authority to make that happen up in here."

Me: "I'm a motherfucking adult now Brain, I own you, I have all the authority I need, now go to sleep."

Brain: "But here's the thing, remember that guy in the dining hall line today, we were waiting on ONE pancake and he came up, asked if we were in line, we said yes, and he had the nerve to shake his head in disgust at us and walk away like the asshole he was."

Me: "He was a nobody, you didn't know him or anything, he was probably just in a shitty mood, because…you know…Afghanistan."

Brain: "Bullshit! Yeah, he's in Afghanistan, but there are pancakes…seriously, it's not that bad…with that stupid ass mustache, we should've knee capped him, you're pathetic." (Brain has a bigger potty mouth than me.)

Me: "Oh, I'm pathetic, don't you mean, WE'RE pathetic."

Brain: "No."

Me: "Shut up and go to sleep."

Brain: "I wanna' climb up a mountain and shout poetry at the goats, and I want to throw a fit when they don't bah back!" she sings at the top of her brain lungs, if brains had lungs. I know, we're getting into tricky territory here.

Me: "OH MY GOD, the goats are in the valleys, not the mountains!"

Brain: "NOT IF THEY'RE MOUNTAIN GOATS! Maybe we should look that up, what kind of goat population Afghanistan has because…"

Me: I cut her off "Don't say another word…I will stick you."

Brain: "I have to go to the bathroom."

Me: "No you don't, we just went."

Brain: "But our stomach hurts, you ate cream cheese AND a tuna melt sandwich in Afghanistan, what did you think was going to happen."

Me: "You're a dirty little liar, you always do this, you say your stomach hurts, I go to the bathroom and, nothing, a fart if I'm lucky. Knock the shit off and go to sleep."

Brain: "You're the one who thought mayonnaise in a third world country was a good idea LAURA, who's the idiot now? Also, we need to call mom, she probably misses us. Social media needs us as well, we didn't platform enough to matter. You had seven cups of coffee today, I wanna' dance! Why was Bukowski like that? I mean, he had that one nice poem about the lady he said he should have helped more, but man, how did his dick NOT fall off? I was also thinking we should take up ballet, I took the liberty of ordering two DVD's off the Internet earlier so we can learn the art of dance. Speaking of online purchases, our panda sweatshirt hasn't come yet. Also, you forgot our daily planner at work so now we can't check things off our list so I'll have to just worry about them instead."

Me: "I hate you."

Brain: "Tell me something I don't know. Hey, we need more face toner, you're looking kind of haggard lately. I like makeup, those tutorials are amazing, contouring is so much easier than I thought it'd be, Kyle'in that shit up allll day long. What exactly is mustard made of, I mean, is it just the seeds of mustard creamed up, or do they add stuff to it, I think they must add something to it."

Me: "What the shit do you even care, we hate mustard, you shit stain."

Brain: "Jesus, I was just curious, calm down, you shouldn't get all ragey right before bed. I told you we should've gotten ahold of some Ambien, so we could be talking to Rue McClanahan right now, I heard that shit is crazy if you don't go right to sleep after taking it. Did you do your kegels today? What year did the Battle of the Bulge happen? I think we should cut our toenails. Also, remember that shitty job we have to go back to once we leave Afghanistan? You know we have to go back to it right, because no one wants to read your stories. This writing thing isn't going to happen. You suck at math. Pretty sure we're going to meet our doom in a Slip n' Slide accident, God those things are terrifying. Again, I gotta' pee, can you get me something to drink, pop, I'd really like a pop."

Me: "We have to get up in five hours, I'm not getting you a soda, I'm warning you I'm going to get the Nyquil."

Brain: "Wait wait wait, no, I have something important to say."

Me: Knowing I'll regret it, "What?"

Brain: "You're going to die alone."

Me: "Thank God!"

Brain: "Anyhow, buenas noches."

Ten minutes later.

Brain: "Mmm, buenas noches, nache, nachos, nachos sound delicious."

# I Don't Want to be Norah Jones Sad Anymore

I'd been on the Negative Nellie train for quite a bit of my life. My whole life really. At any point in time, I can be found ranting about something, in the hopes that the something will stop existing. Guess what, this doesn't work.

I could scream at people with a blow horn at every grocery store parking lot I came across, but fully abled people would still leave their ducking, yes I said ducking, because that's what you're doing, you're ducking actual human responsibility bestowed upon you as a mouth breather, and I hate you for putting the carts exactly adjacent to the cart corral, instead of IN IT.

Some inconvenient, or annoying scenario will always bother me. Something had to give. The burden of being annoyed was getting too heavy and frankly, I wanted clearer skin, free from so much stress.

There are more things in the world than I could ever hope to loathe, so I just had to figure out how to deal with it all. I got to a point where I decided to try an experiment. Every time something bothered me, I tried to imagine how that exact thing is really a good thing. I'm not reinventing the wheel here, I'm just putting twenty twen-twens on it (that's a rap phrase for expensive car rims in case you didn't know).

Here's just a few scenarios I've come up with so far in turning bad things into good things:

When you put your socks on after cutting your toenails, and it hurts because you cut them too short.

The bad: Really toes, really? You're gonna' punk out on me and hurt BECAUSE I PUT SOCKS ON YOU? After I dress my feet carefully, I say, "Ooo, that stings…ma' toes are sensitive." I walk around, spontaneously jumping and breathing hard because I dragged the sock material across my toes a tad too hard for my baby-ass newly cut toes to handle. Get it together toes.

The good: I'm beyond grateful I can bend over enough to cut my toenails because not everyone can. My dad developed a huge beer belly later in life, surprisingly because he quit drinking beer and ate food instead, so he couldn't reach his own feet to clip his nails.

Guess who had that job?

He'd yell from the living room, "Hey, Laura, come cut my toenails." Then, I'd crawl into the living room brandishing a paper brown grocery bag ripped in two pieces. One piece was to put on the floor for the clippings to fall on, the other, as a shield for my face, since the nails never actually fell to the floor. They were so thick and long that they more or less shot at my eyeballs like rockets as I clipped down on the nails. The process was basically like using bolt cutters on someone's toes. Dad always gave me money after, which only made it feel grosser somehow.

So yeah, it's pretty great I can do that shit myself. In the long run, I can deal with the sensitive toes so long as I can bend over to do it myself.

That weird noise people make on the phone after you're done talking to them as you prepare to hang up.

The bad: I'm on the phone and saying my goodbyes to the person on the other end.

"Ok, sounds good, I'll see you tomorrow."

"Yep, see you tomorrow...ehyum bye."

"Uh-hum, bye."

What the shit is that whole transaction even called? It's always a random guttural acknowledgement that the conversation is officially over and for whatever reason I silently curse myself after saying it once I hang up. I don't know why I cater to people and follow suit by saying, "Yeeeahum, bye," right back at them. Occasionally I'll get caught up in a loop and do it exactly seven times back and forth until I slam the phone down in defiance, "THIS IS OVER!" Use your words, not just sounds.

The good: This whole phenomenon gives me a chance to be creative in phone conversations. Instead of just grunting goodbye on the phone, I can make grand statements that are poignant and final.

I'll yell at them and hang up before the other person can say anything else. Or, I will loudly sing, "Whoop whoop...this is da' police," or "Long distance rates DO

NOT apply," and my favorite, a banshee warrior cry of, "I have been given nothing….Go earn that Klondike bar," and I will drop the phone on the floor. I have yet to employ these tactics, but the ahem days are numbered.

# Derivative of My Integral

I followed a boy to college. I bet you can't guess how it turned out. That's a lie, you're probably most positively right about what you think happened.

In high school, I always assumed I'd go to college, despite my family residing on the lower rung of the middle-class ladder. I wouldn't say my parents looked me dead in the eyes and said I could climb higher, but I got the feeling it was possible. I would have to pull my own weight though. They always stressed grades and if I happened to pull a B in some class, they were inevitably disappointed and I would stress eat the pain away.

"What happened?" my mom asked, looking at my report card as dad stood behind her. I had A's in every other class besides math. They wanted to know why I got a B in math class. Oh I don't know, because I didn't give two shits what any particular triangle was called, nor did the thought of cosigns keep me up at night. My parents told me I would just have to work harder, stay after class for four days instead of three that month.

I consider myself relatively intelligent, but if my brain doesn't want to learn something or hang onto a tidbit, it's not happening. Math was my worst subject.

"Ok brain, we need to remember how to find the properties of derivatives and the integrals of some stuff," I'd say. "Apparently, this comes from the summation of infinitesimal differences." What this means is, there are an infinite amount of ways you can mess that shit up.

I thought, "Yeah no, in no way shape or form, curves or not, is this shit integral to me functioning as a person who succeeds in life and gets laid, just, nope."

It was hard to show my work when I had blurry cry goggles on because I couldn't figure equations out. My hair always covered my face as I leaned over the paper, a la The Ring, snot dripping onto my graph paper.

I'm not sure how any of my math book survived a single semester with me because of my rage at not understanding most concepts. Homework sessions usually ended with me literally putting teeth marks in the covers after biting them, and then throwing the books down the stairs. I'm sure I looked like a mad Wildling gone off the deep end, leaning over our banister in the dark stairway, screaming at the book at the bottom, "YOU KNOW NOTHING NEWTON, YOU SON-OF-A-BITCH, YOU."

Today, I wish I knew back then that it was not a big deal, the grades that is. Indiana University probably would've admitted me with a C average. It was the only school I applied to. I had gone to a college fair my senior year of high school, and shortly considered going to St. Olaf College on the singular fact that Rose Nylund from The Golden Girls came from St. Olaf, Minnesota, and if everyone was as dumb as the show made them seem, I was set. I'd probably be able to get my Doctorate in that case. Then I thought how cold it would get there in winter and decided that was a no. All the different university pamphlets sat in my book bag for weeks.

My on-again, off-again high school boyfriend at the time, Tony, told me he was going to IU. He casually mentioned the school had a good Social Work program. I'd be good at that he said, because I was a nice person so I should go there.

So, I did.

I knew people who planned their bathroom breaks more than I planned for college. Late one night, I sat at my dial-up computer in the hallway, waiting for the school website to load. I wanted to find out more about what social work really was. I read something along the lines of helping people and high fived myself, I was going to be a Social Worker. I applied for a few scholarships and got one for minorities. Being half Puerto Rican paid off. For the application, I made up some story of feeling discriminated against. Well, I didn't make it up, it happened, but I never actually felt discriminated against. It was a tale about someone once telling me they didn't believe that different races should mix, not even realizing I was technically one of the outcomes of such a crazy concept, and that person drove me to school most of my high school years. To hear her say that she didn't believe in races mixing was a silent nod to resenting that I existed. I knew she didn't mean it that way and we are friends to this day, but it still hurt and I guess the story stuck enough with me to earn $10,000 a year in scholarship money. Yay for racism!

People ask me all the time what I am.

"Shit, just a lonely, single sapien I guess, what do you mean?" I generally replied. My hooded eyes and curly hair confused the crap out of people. For me, my genetic makeup only concerns me in the fact that I'm more likely to be a drunk because of my father. Let me clarify here, not because he was Puerto Rican, but because he was an alcoholic, which means I was roughly four times as likely to become one myself. I was more likely to be an alcoholic than someone who didn't have a parent who sat at the kitchen table, holding their head and hangover together with their hands and told their little girl to please not make so much noise playing with their pink Barbie shower play set because it hurt daddy's head. Little did I know, I'd get out of that tiny kitchen in New Jersey and end up at a legit accredited college, where, quite frankly, people weren't much smarter than pub regulars, thirty years down the bottle's neck.

Months after applying to college, I got the acceptance letter. I couldn't tell you what it said except that I got in. I applied for loans, which I subsequently spent on a lot of beer, burritos and coffee, and am still paying back. I'm not sure what I would've done if IU had rejected me. I'd probably still be working at my local grocery store, my soul would be more depleted from years of asking customers if they'd checked their eggs as I beeped their items through, and customers would continue to yell at me to get my pen off the weight scale as I weighed their bananas. Hey, COUPON GUY, that pen probably only added a good ten cents, and although now as a spending adult, I understand your anger, you didn't have to be such a twat about it.

Sadly, the customer service experience is gone now. I literally used to interrogate customers as a cashier; "How are you, did you find everything, do you have any coupons, would you like paper or plastic, do you have a store card, do you need help out to your car?" I'd throw obscenities under my breath when they refused to say, "Have a nice day," back at me after I threw it out there.

Now, there are never any lanes open with actual cashiers and you must checkout yourself. This never translates to lower prices, just weekly traumatizing events at the grocery store. DON'T YOU TRY TO TELL ME WHEN I CAN OR CAN'T PUT MY ITEMS IN THE CART, THERE'S NOTHING ON THE FUCKING BELT YOU PIECE OF SHIT MACHINE, I'M GOING TO DESTROY YOU AND ALL THE MACHINE BABIES IN YOUR FUCKING CODED DNA THAT WILL COME IN THE FUTURE, IN FACT, I MIGHT GO AHEAD AND TRANSPORT BACK IN TIME AND FIND THE CREATER OF AUTOMATATED CHECKOUTS AND…WELL I'M NOT GOING TO THREATEN HIS OR HER DEATH BUT I WOULD DISTRACT THEM TO THE POINT WITH THE SEX STUFF SO THEY DON'T HAVE TIME TO CREATE THEM… DO YOU THINK I'M PLAYING, SUPERMARKET INDUSTRY? These self-serve registers are tearing the country apart at the seams. Seriously, where are fourteen-year-olds supposed to work when all the adults are taking over McDonald's because our nation suffers from a crippling inequality in wealth disbursement and rising costs of higher education?

Come to think of it, besides my nieces, I don't think I've uttered a single word to a teenager in about five years and I wonder how they're supposed to learn about social interaction with adults, other than their parents, if they can't get jobs at local grocery stores.

Back to the start of my first semester at college, I followed Tony to Bloomington. I never thought we'd end up together, but I followed him around the campus because none of my other high school friends were going to that college. He was a face I recognized in the crowd of blondes and size two jeans. I still loved him, but he loved redheads who pretended to be religious but bought leopard underwear just like the rest of us.

I remember standing out on the curb in front of my dorm the first night I was on my own. It felt significant, but more like a joke. It felt like at any second a grownup was going to poke their head around a tree and tell me to go back to my room as they pushed their glasses back up on their nose. I waited for someone to tell me I shouldn't eat pasta for the 17th time that week.

No one told me to go to bed that night.

For the first time in my life, no one else owned my actions. It felt like my body leaned forward at an angle to the concrete sidewalk, twilight darkening, itching to take off at a sprint in an undetermined direction. There was nowhere I was told to be. Tony introduced me to Ahriman that night and we went for pizza or Chinese food, I don't remember. Oh yeah, Red was there, she was Tony's girlfriend by that point. Well praise Jesus.

I wanted to punch Red right in her freckly face for stealing Tony away in high school when they both went to an academy that my parents wouldn't agree to let me go to.

During the first year at college, I pined after him for a few semesters until one night, I saw he was studying Hebrew and I thought it was such a silly thing. Not because Hebrew is silly in and of itself, but to me, it just wasn't a very practical thing, and at the time I was a very practical girl. If it had happened now, I think I would have fallen in love with him a little bit more. I remember, he didn't understand something in the text he was reading and he snapped at me when I asked a question. Still remembering the last blowjob I gave him, I stared at his face and with a stroke of his pen drawing a symbol, I ceased to love him anymore. It fell away like after you come in out of the snow and you drop your wet jeans at the entrance. Your toes are clammy, but feel so much better now, warm and alive, and you'd rather just throw the jeans out than wait for them to dry because they'd always be just a little bit hard at the bottoms because of the salt, no matter how dry they became. Tony was dried out and salty in my eyes that night.

I eventually stopped talking to Tony altogether around sophomore year, because at some point he told me I should kill myself. I don't even remember what I'd done to make him angry. I don't remember a lot from that time.

I resented the idea that I was paying an establishment damn near $30,000 a year in tuition, only to have that establishment tell me I needed to take more math classes which had no relation to Social Work as a major.

"But why tho'?" I'd ask my career counselor.

She would reply with, "Because."

"Well I don't see how statistics has anything to do with me being able to help a victim of domestic violence create a safety plan for leaving their abusive partner because in all reality, that is the most dangerous time and generally, a victim has to try eight times to leave someone before it sticks."

She'd roll her eyes and sing, "Dolla dolla bills ya'll, blah blah, well-rounded, blah blah, we charge you so much because we have a basketball team that regularly makes it to the March Madness finals, yada yada, we have to pay for that somehow, shut up and take all the MATHS."

At this rate, I will be debt free in about 2030 is what I'm guessing.

# When a Man Hates a Woman

One thing Boyfriend never understood about our relationship was my tendency to shut down during arguments. Many times, in the middle of a fight, my mouth would clamp shut and my head would go down as I zoned out of that plane of existence. He'd call me out on the fact that I flinched when he would simply grab a cup or something involving raising his arm. That same flinch I still haven't been able to make go away. Sometimes I forget why it ever existed in the first place.

A couple years ago, I was full stride in my 'cleanout everything' mode. I went through all my belongings on the main floors of the house and it was time to go through the hidden, tucked away memories. I brought down plastic bins and cardboard boxes from the attic. They were filled with childhood and college memorabilia I was finally ready to get rid of.

The boxes also contained decade-old photos of friends and way too many photos of me stuffing my face at various birthday parties, attended by people I no longer spoke to.

I looked through the pictures in awe of how beautiful I was.

If you know me, you know that's completely out of character for me to say, because I've always been more of the self-deprecating type. I know, the whole bit solely exists so I can pretend that I'm fine with the idea that I'm not fine and sucking at life, but hey, at least I'm making fun of myself before anyone else can so there's that.

One photo showed me standing in the surf on a beach in Puerto Rico. I had on a blue tankini with white flowers on it. It was taken the summer after I graduated high school. I had smooth, lightly tanned skin. My freckles looked cute, before freckles were a fad and people got them tattooed on their faces, which I think is still a thing that people do, kind of like wearing glasses even when their eye site is perfect. My hair had honest-to-Lord Zod, beach waves that floated around my face, and I had curvy thighs to die for.

These days, I am under no pretense that the years have not been kind to the body bag I carry all my organs around in.

The lines in my forehead are now frozen in a permanent frown, my thighs and ass are dimpled with all the sugar and fat I consume daily, and if I don't suck in my stomach, I most certainly cannot see my feet if I glance straight down.

My younger, hotter self was only concerned with whether my eyeliner was running and spending my college loan money on new corset tops at tween clothing stores supplied by slave labor. My proudest moments were of not getting vomit on said new top at the previous night's frat party.

My older self is proud of using a day off to get an oil change, or spending my weekends at the grocery store at midnight, specifically to buy a new nightgown. Have I mentioned I'm a 32 year-old-woman yet, and not 70?

I admired the photos, but didn't long for what once was and will never be again. I eventually put the photos aside.

In the very bottom of the last bin was a black, leather-bound journal.

I sat amongst the other items on the floor and began to read it. I flipped through the pages, not at all certain this had been MY journal. I thought there was no way I was that depressed and emotional as a young adult.

Every entry consisted of musings about my current relationship at the time, specifically with Ahriman.

"It's my fault…everything mean he did was my fault…I don't know why I'm the way I am, I'm so tired but I can't sleep. He was supposed to call me but he didn't and the last time we talked, it didn't go very well."

My 18-year-old self in that journal was more annoying than the most heinous protagonist in the latest YA novel, bleeding our society of strong female lead characters. I absolutely hated the girl whose thoughts I was reading.

This young, once vibrant girl believed to her very core that Ahriman hit her because she was too fat and not beautiful enough. She believed it and believed it until it dulled her to less than a person with thoughts and feelings and ideas and love and compassion.

She convinced herself that this man, boy really, made her sleep on his dorm room floor every night, not because he was a certifiable psychopath, but because he loved her and just wanted to be closer to her.

I thought to the time he grabbed that girl by the wrist, and spun her around to face the mirror. He had to make her see who she was for her own good; her frizzy hair and ugly freckles, her yellow tooth that got knocked out in high school, her "saggy tits", her fat thighs painted with stretch marks. Most importantly, he had to point out her blubbery stomach. He told her she was worse than nothing, she was lacking. He had to point these things out so she would realize that, despite all those faults, he loved her and no one else would because of them.

This wonderful girl was living in a Hallmark movie gone bad, minus the dog, minus the Santa hat at Christmas and minus B celebrities. She didn't even know it.

Through college, she sat in her social work classes, learning about the cycle of violence and how abusive partners groomed their victims to put up with the pain, how they manipulated them. That girl would go home at night and write in her journal about wishing she didn't wake up in the morning. Every night, on the floor she was in tears praying to God. She asked not to wake up, that's all, nothing more, nothing less.

Then the morning came and she would roll up her sleeping blankets in his room, sore from the previous nights' argument, and go to class numb and disappointed she had opened her eyes for another day.

The first time he hit her, she thought it was her fault because she should not have been drinking with friends. If she hadn't been drunk, he wouldn't have dragged her to his room, shutting the door in her friends' face. If she hadn't been drunk, he wouldn't have turned to her, hand cocked back in the air, calling her a stupid little bitch.

Luckily, the alcohol abated the pain of the clap of his hand to her face.

She barely felt him pull her hair and climb on top of her. It was the fear that made her scream out, not the pain. But if she just would've kept quiet, he wouldn't have had to shove his fingers down her throat, gagging and silencing her yelp. It was her fault for flailing back at him, swallowing blood from where his nails scratched the inside of her esophagus. He had to wrap his hands around her throat until she laid still and stopped fighting.

She left his room and a couple of guys stopped her because she was crying. They had been drinking too, so her mumbled "Okays" were all they needed to send her on her way.

Weeks later, she had met a new friend, Jeff, who made her smile. She made a mistake though, she shouldn't have gone to the gym with Jeff. Ahriman had followed her to the gym and saw Jeff there too. She parted ways with Jeff and Ahriman found her. She tried to talk to him, to tell him she was just taking a dance class, but he shoved her away from him and into a wall in the lobby. Someone saw the shove and told a staff member what he'd seen. Then, a man who worked there approached the girl and Ahriman and asked if she was ok, then turned to Ahriman and told him to leave. She followed him like a lost kitten, scared of following, but more scared of being left behind. Later, in the dorm room, she was the stupid one who fell when Ahriman pushed her against a metal bed frame, and she hit her back. Why did she have to make him do those things, she asked herself, she had gotten him in trouble.

Another time, Ahriman was trying to study, but the girl wanted a break and asked to go to her own room. He said no, he needed her to be there so he could concentrate and not wonder what she was doing. He then kicked her in the ribs.

It was even her fault, two years later when he raped her.

She had been so strong before, when she left him. Two friends and one of her professors had staged an intervention. Jessica let her stay at her apartment until the end of the school year.

A few days after leaving him, Ahriman caught her outside of the dorm. She was silent as she shook her head at him, no, she wasn't going to go with him. Jessica was there, her champion. Jessica stood watch, with nothing but her friendship to guard the girl. He eventually walked away, and it sanded her heart down to the base.

But that girl bumped into him at a bar two years later. Drunk and brazen, she stared him in the face in the dark and told him she wasn't scared of him anymore because she was joining the Army and would be stronger than he ever would be.

As I read the words of the journal, I couldn't believe this unrecognizable girl. I screamed at the girl to not trust him. The girl believed him when he told her he would drive her home from the bar.

But first, he wanted her to see his apartment on campus.

Numbing fear washed over her as Ahriman took a left instead of a right, going the opposite direction from her dorm. He told her he would take her home "after." He gave her a tour of his apartment and tried to make her go to his bedroom but she planted her feet. She ran outside but he caught her and convinced her to go back inside. All she had to do was lay down and then he would take her home.

He called her a dirty little whore as he was on top of her. He spit in her mouth as he forced himself inside her and asked her if her boyfriend would like that someone else was fucking her. She didn't struggle; she just lay there, whispering "no." It never occurred to her to call the police. What would she say? There were no marks on her and she was drunk, she couldn't afford a lawyer. His family had money. She'd be asked about her sexual partners and how much she drank on occasions. She would be asked why she didn't fight him. She had no answer for why she didn't. She carried on once he dropped her off at home, too scared to tell her boyfriend what had happened.

I closed the journal and dropped it back into the bottom of the storage bin.

I spoke to Ahriman online a couple of times after I graduated college. Last I heard, he said he was thinking about going to New York or somewhere else to become a fashion runway model. Did I mention the professor in the intervention said he had clear signs of a certifiable sociopath?

When a career in high fashion didn't work out, I saw he came up with an energy drink in California. There were pictures and everything of the fancy bro launch party, though I can't remember what the drink was called.

Back in my living room, I turned towards the couch, kneeling. Bent over, I clenched and unclenched my small hands around a throw pillow. I swayed my body in a calming ritual of movement. I attacked the couch, full of scorching rage. I wrenched the pillow over my head and slammed it over and over onto the couch cushions. The pillow flung out of my hands so I pounded my empty fists on the dark red leather. My entire body thrashed around with every blow, as the rest of the house remained silent. I returned every slap, kick, choke and every insult, every "cunt…bitch…" and "whore." Spit flung from my mouth as I thrashed at the couch.

My vision went black and my mind vibrated from the outburst.

I tipped my head back and one shriek escaped me, just one.

Then, I stopped and wiped the snot and tears from my face. Gasping, I stood up. I was damp with sweat and tears. I swayed back and forth on my feet for a good five minutes.

I started to laugh hysterically. It was four o'clock in the morning, and I was alone in my home. My home I paid for, my home that I made, my home that I lived in.

My shoulders shook, and I smiled. I remembered the braces on Ahriman's teeth, I remembered his bulging eyes and his thinning hair, and I remembered his general affinity for hermaphrodite porn.

Don't misunderstand me, there's nothing wrong with hermaphrodite porn if that's what you like, but he was so ashamed of liking it. One night after watching it with him, because hey, I'm a team player, his face changed into an angry cringe and he told me to never tell anyone about it.

That night, years later, I laughed. I laughed because of all the things to be ashamed of, of all his transgressions; liking hermaphrodite porn was the least of his worries.

So, to any man in my future, I have this to say to you: That is why I flinch when you are angry. Not because I think you would hit me, not because you've given me any indication that you will kick me when I am down, but because of all the other times someone else I loved did.

# Farts of Fury

Note: I really debated on this 'story', yeah, that's what we'll go with, 'story," because it's lowbrow comedy. I decided these parts of what made life bearable in an otherwise sad state of affairs, was worth sharing.

A lot of people track the history of their lives in firsts. They tick off first steps, first words, first love, first house, first child, first orgasm. I mostly graph my history in farts. I know, I know, this is such a silly and gross thing to talk about. No self-respecting lady would do that, or should do that. This is literature and it should be serious and have no mention of flatulence, past or present.

"Please spare us," I can hear you saying.

I really tried not to write about the following anecdotes, because I'm in a phase right now, where it's important for me to figure out my feminine wiles, so I can use them for evil. Farts don't exactly add to the persona of being a delicate orchid that is good at seduction. In theory, boys are supposed to have no idea I even have a colon, let alone pass gas. Boyfriend knew I farted, oh, he kneeew.

Here's the thing though, my family is basically a fartbox philharmonic symphony. This makes me mostly comfortable with my natural bodily functions. Some people like cat videos, others laugh at dad jokes. For me, farting is one of the constants in my life I can absolutely depend on to make me laugh, so, yeah, if that makes me immature and gross, I'm fine with it.

The first time I ever remember farting in front of someone other than family, I was in preschool. I have no idea how old that would make me, and I'm not doing the math but it's also one of the ONLY clear memories I have of being a miniature me.

My entire class was taken on a bathroom break and the trip had to be orchestrated like a tactical maneuver. You can't just tell a five-year-old to have at it and motion them out into the wilderness that is the hallways, where they have to fend for themselves. If one child went, more would want to follow and before you knew it, it'd be anarchy and little kids would be peeing and pooping on anything and everything, and there are not enough teacher's aides in the world to contain that.

So, to avoid catastrophe, we all lined up outside the classroom with supervision, and went through the motions, as if on a conveyer belt towards the bathrooms. When we were finished doing our business, we all lined back up in the hall into two columns, quietly. That day, I had the prettiest white lace southern bell dress on, and I admired it as I stood there. I looked down past my little belly to the skirt of the dress thinking, "Damn, just look at that poof, it's so freaking poofed I can't even right now, I am looking fabulous with my poof."

I was zoned out, digging myself, so I almost didn't hear Ms. Hanna kneel behind me and say something in my ear.

"Laura, your dress is tucked into your underwear, pull it out right now," she scolded. I turned to Nick, who was standing behind us. Bend down right behind my shoulder,

Ms. Hanna told Nick not to look at my butt while I straightened myself out.

I was so angry, angry that this lady implied I smooshed the back of my dress into my underwear on purpose and now she was mad at me. Just as she was about to stand back up from behind me, I straight tooted in her face. It kind of went "beerp." She gasped in shock while still kneeling back there and her eyes were huge when I turned around and looked her dead in the eyes. A couple other kids heard and giggled with delight.

"Laura," she said with her mouth open in awe. Now that I think about it, it probably got in her mouth. Sorry not sorry.

"What?" I asked, and turned around to face forward without waiting for a reply.

I wouldn't say I tried to fart in her face, but I will say I didn't hold it in either. I wasn't embarrassed at all, which I can't say how I'd feel if this happened at my current age. I'd like to think I would do the exact same thing. This was all before I knew farts were funny and how much power they had. Grandpa hadn't even taught me how the "Pull My Finger Game," worked at Thanksgiving dinners. I'm here to tell you my friends, that is genetics at its finest, it was ingrained in my very being.

Now, farting on planes is another story. Some people hate traveling on airplanes, but they're a haven for me. I am content to sit and do nothing productive for the whole flight. There is literally nothing else I should or could be doing at that point. Some people get annoyed with the pleasantry of preflight checks, but I get super calm when I watch stewardesses do their thing and explain how seat belts work. I'm also hopped up on Benadryl, because, yeah, Benadryl. On one flight, I got a little too relaxed though. I was listening to music with my headphones in and accidently let a fart pop out. Immediately, in a state of panic, my eyes flitted back and forth to the people sitting next to me, the rest of my body clenched. DID THEY HEAR, DID THEY HEAR, I DON'T KNOW IF THEY HEARD, THE MUSIC MUFFLED IT, OH MY GOD, IT DIDN'T JUST SLIDE OUT, IT JUMPED OUT AND I HAVE NO IDEA HOW LOUD IT WAS. Then I prayed to every last one of my ancestors that it didn't smell.

"Please Gregoria, don't let it smell." I then sweated the entire rest of the flight, waiting for one of the passengers to wrinkle their nose and wave their hands in front of their noses. Fortunately, that never happened. I'm not sure why I'm only embarrassed about farts when they happen on airplanes, but not out in the open.

My mom though, she is a master of flatulence. I mean, of course she is, because she learned from the Grand Master, my grandpa.

Not long ago, I was sitting with mom, eating dinner on a TV tray in the living room. I was on the couch and mom sat in a recliner to my right. I brought a fork to my mouth when a sharp, squeaky sound vibrated from the left of me. It legitimately startled me and I jumped. I thought a mouse or something crawled behind the couch. I turned and looked back at mom on the right of me and she was laughing.

"What's wrong, Laura?" she asked. I looked at her betrayed, it was HER, she had farted.

I said, "But, it came from the left of me….you, you're on my right, you just…when did you learn how to throw your farts?" I asked angrily. I still have yet to grasp this gift of sorcery farts she has.

She's sneaky like that. Another time, we drove to the bank and I rode in the passenger seat, just along for the ride. We pulled up to the drive-through deposit lane. I sat there anxious, only in the way people are anxious when the one thing more boring and tedious than filling out a bank deposit slip and awkwardly placing it in the space tube thing is watching someone else fill out their bank deposit slip and send it up the tube.

I watched mom as she reached out of her window and leaned over to place the container in the shoot. Immediately, "breepeebebebeeee," came out of her ass. I didn't stop clutching my sides in laughter until we got all the way home.

Then, there was the fart that genuinely made me fear for my life.

I grew up in the house right next to my grandparents. It was nice they were only a few feet away and I saw them often. Grandpa had gone deer hunting that day and was out in the garage with his kill and mom was there too, congratulating him. The garage door was up, so I could see them both when I came home from doing whatever it is a teenager does. I got out of my car and walked up to the garage to talk to them as the deer hung from the rafters, half skinned.

At any given time, grandpa could be seen slaughtering various animals out back. Seeing a trail of blood run through the alley was not strange to us. In the dead of night, you could find him carrying black plastic jumbo trash bags out to the garbage bins. It's only a little weird to think grandpa could have been a successful serial killer my whole life, and I would've had no idea. Meh, it was just turtle, squirrel or deer guts, probably, maybe, not sure.

We all stood there for a while, chatting about how much the deer weighed and all that other normal stuff you say about dead animals. The chatter became quiet and behind me, I heard a deep menacing growl sound coming from behind me. Naturally, my survival instincts kicked in so I sprawled my arms into the air, and leaped about five feet further into the garage to get away from whatever animal had emitted the growl. I was certain a rabid dog or wolf had smelled the fresh meat and was moving in for brunch. Mind you, I live on literal Main Street, so the chances of there being a wild animal were close to nil. But in my head, the monster was going to murder every one of us to get to the deer. Now, an upstanding person would have tried to shield their loved ones from the wild beast, but that person wasn't me that day. I chose self-preservation as I ran away from the noise.

My immediate thought was, "I don't want to die!" I turned to look behind me, ready to see mom and grandpa torn to shreds.

Turns out, they weren't being mauled after all. Mom put her hands on her hips and grandpa looked confused. They had no idea why I had jumped, and neither did I anymore because there was no wild animal ready to pounce. I scanned my surroundings and it sunk in, the growl I heard was not a growl, it was grandpa's trumpeting ass.

I clenched my fists and said, "I thought there was a dog or something, growling." They remained silent for a moment.

I walked out of the garage and went home next door, all the while hearing both of them howl with laughter. I had confused a fart for a growl. I shouldn't beat myself up though, I now know I got cat like reflexes and that story still makes me laugh.

# Bwaha Moment

Just an FYI here, there's going to be quite a few F-bombs thrown in this one.

For a five-year span of my life I was convinced that if I read the right article in a magazine, I would one day finally figure out some things and have an "AHA" moment a la' Oprah. I would crush Boyfriend's hands as I jumped up and down on our couch, I would scream and shout how much I was in love with me, myself and I, because I found myself by reading an enlightening article that made gluten free, coconut flake covered rhinestones shit out of my ass.

If I ever had an actual AHA moment like so many other women out there, I don't think it would be so refined. It would be more of a BWAHA moment, because really, all good things start with B's...boobs, boys, beds, bathtubs and belly button fuzz, just to name a few. And BWAHA has a more, oh shit look what I've done feeling to it.

I read hundreds of magazines to no avail, but I was sure that if the stars aligned just right, I would be at the grocery store and my eyes would fall upon the exact magazine I was meant to find. I'd become the next revolutionary leader because "The Secret" had finally been unlocked in my head by reading about various sex positions that would change my life. It could totally happen.

I imagined the right headline would jump out at me, among all the tabloids of celebrity cellulite and who's banging who. I would see a Time magazine, and it would have a picture with some important person standing on some important object implying a social uprising. I imagined I'd see the right headline on some other magazine, I'd buy the magazine, take it home and stuff it in my workbag until I'd decided to read it once my boss left the office. Angels would sing, bells would chime, and I'd discover how to be the 'best me', or I would learn how to de-clutter my closet forever. Then I would be happy for the rest of my life.

In an ideal world, Runner's World would teach me how to prevent my tits from hurting while running as they bounced. Yoga Journal would teach me how to meditate in order to keep from wanting to punch 17-year-olds at my gym, walking around with their young spry vaginas. Glamour would show why those LouieLouiebatons cost a thousand dollars by deconstructing the shoes in a photo layout and reveal they use baby dolphin skin for the insoles (I'm pretty sure they don't use baby dolphin skins in their shoes, but you can never tell). But no, instead I buy O Magazine, showing me all the superfluous shit I didn't even know I needed.

Women's Health tried to teach me how to get flat abs without doing a single sit-up. They told me about all the things I SHOULD eat. But what they failed to mention is, to have flat abs you also need to not eat five cheese Danishes in the span of three days. Sure, they tell you to eat right, but they make no mention of specifically NOT ordering a 20 ounce steak from Texas Roadhouse because the two rolls you ate smothered in cinnamon butter didn't quite hit the spot while you were waiting on your Grandpa and his girlfriend to show up. These are the things I need, detailed accounts of every single unhealthy thing I could possibly do, and I need to be told not to do them.

Marie Clair taught me that fashion was important, but not as important as knowing what various horrible fates awaited my lady parts, either from strangers prowling deserted offices, or the threat lurking within the vag, i.e. yeast infections, bacterial vaginitis, or even more terrifying, chlamydia, which is surprisingly still around.

Better Homes and Gardens showed me how to turn a tree trunk into a vanity table as well as how to plant the perfect bulb to grow the tree trunk I would need thirty years later to build the vanity table. BHG showed me what my house should look like, but I'm pretty sure Better Homes and Gardens never had to contend with dog turds the size of soccer balls in their yards either. BHG doesn't consider the fact that real people live in my house and they eat snacks and take dumps, not always in that order. The homes in that fucking magazine showcase houses where, I assure you, no one has ever taken an explosive shit, thrown up purple liquid after two bottles of wine, and they never had a dog that vomited inside the confines of the home.

Eventually, after pouring over shiny pages, I finally had my BWAHA moment.

I was at my desk at work skimming through a magazine aimed at living a simple life. The editors talked about people who went to brunch and cleaned their fridges…like with soap. Did you know there are supposedly people who take everything out of the refrigerator, and I shit you not, they use soap and water to clean the refrigerator doors and drawers, or crispers as they're technically called.

I'm pretty sure that's the antitheses of simple. I, myself choose to simply NOT clean my refrigerator. This magazine advised women to not sweat the small stuff, like when their crystal stemware has spots on it, it's not a big deal they say, Sarah won't care.

Really, crystal stemware, huh?

I know for a fact, I don't live in the 50's anymore and my glassware comes from Wal-Mart, or Target if I'm feeling fancy. I do have a pint glass I'm fond of. I stole it from a bar in college, but I think spots give it character. At one time, I also owned 33 plastic beer pitchers from a St. Paddy's Day tent party. Hey, they had a hole in the fence and left those 33 pitchers unsupervised, what else was I supposed to do besides sneak them into my trunk?

Simple magazine, fuck you and your crystal stemware.

This same 'simple' magazine had an ad page; for what I don't know, but it had an ad depicting a mother in the kitchen…she had one kid, who was wearing rain boots. The model used one hand to balance the toddler on the kitchen counter, and with the other hand she was holding a rolling pin. Flour was everywhere, along with ingredients for an incredible recipe she was making. There was a ridiculously long to-do list pasted to the fridge. What got me was the mother was wearing this fancy bright red satiny cocktail dress and bright shiny heels while doing all this. She had a beautiful pinned up hairstyle, only slightly tousled.

That was where I lost it completely, a satin red dress and baking was thrown in my face and I was having none of it.

Who wears that shit while cooking dinner? It obviously failed as an ad campaign because I don't even know what it was advertising. I knew I'd seen that type of shenanigans before in other media and entertainment outlets, but this shit was ridiculous.

In the second Sex and the City movie, Charlotte goes bat shit crazy because she's wearing some beautiful cream-colored skirt suit while baking cupcakes and her horrible daughter has red icing on her hands and wipes them on Charlotte's ass. Charlotte goes and cries in the pantry because her vintage skirt is ruined. I have an idea Charlotte, how about you don't wear expensive irreplaceable clothing while making cupcakes? Now, Carrie can do that shit all day long because she doesn't have tiny people spewing fluids from every orifice on her.

It's got to stop, this idea that women have to look like Julia Roberts walking the red carpet while working an oven. And it all makes me feel like garbage that I don't own any skirt suits. Did we learn nothing from Julia Childs? That lady, when she cooked, she wore the shit out of a button-down shirt and had an apron handy.

Right then, at my desk, I decided magazines could go fuck themselves. I went home to my kitchen, took my pants off, whipped up a bowl of cereal from a box, and added chocolate chips for flair.

I don't need a magazine telling me how to spice up my fellatio repertoire, nor do I need them making me feel inferior because I have no intention of cooking a meal requiring grated truffles…what the hell is a truffle anyways? I always thought it was a special chocolate, but I also have a distinct feeling it's a fungus of some sort that only rich people eat. They probably taste awful, but they're expensive, so you know they're good.

I'll tell you what's clear and simple, magazines don't offer advice for the real world.

The people who make these magazines, I don't think they exist in the world that their readers do. They live in Manhattan apartments and they pay people to do all the things they tell us we should be doing. They quite possibly have terrible relationships with their husbands because the police have been called to their condos for domestic disputes, because an argument exploded over pillow placements.

"Ted, why did you throw the couch pillows on the floor?" Linda would ask her husband.

"I wanted to sit on the couch, Linda," husband says.

"That pillow you threw on the floor was $300. Did you forget we don't sit on the couch, Ted. That's not what it's for."

"Eat a dick Linda."

Or, the editors and creators could have wonderful lives, I hope they do, but I doubt it.

I'm not perfect, I still buy magazines when I'm in airports, and occasionally when I feel like I need to take a trip to fantasyland. I just wish there were better options.

There's no shortage of publications online and in certain stores, but the readily available options are all the same.

I have an idea for you mainstream magazine publishers. Instead of teaching me how to get wine stains out of my carpet, here's a few things I'd prefer you cover.

Is it safe to keep my period panties with the rest of my underwear or is it like a plague that spreads to my other underwear and soon all my panties are period panties?

How do I clean a dog's crusty brown eye boogers off my cream walls? Because seriously, it's like he walks down the halls, and rubs his face on them.

If I clean a glass that's used for rinsing after I brush my teeth, with the same sponge I use to clean the toilet seat, will rinsing the glass with mouthwash negate the grossness of that situation, or do I absolutely need to have a different sponge?

Realistically, how many days can I go wearing the same pair of socks without getting a foot fungus?

How does one look graceful while picking up their dog's shit on walks...also, how do I get him to refrain from doing it on the busiest street in my neighborhood where everyone can drive by and watch me with a baggie on my hand. Do I need to be dressed up for this or can I wear sweatpants and should I wave and smile to everyone, with the poop bag in my hand?

If I leave raw pork tenderloin out to thaw, but forget to put it back in the fridge before bed, and when I wake up, it's kind of sort of warm…can I just cook it anyways and hope for the best as long as the smell doesn't make me gag?

Should I worry about the dog's dingleberries getting on the leather couch, and if said berries do get on it, are Lysol wipes adequate enough to wipe it off?

Am I missing something about the whole concept of Spanx? I don't think I'm doing Spanx right. I put those suckers on and yes, they make my lower belly a tad smoother, but then they smash the fat up to the top of my belly, so a roll spills over the top of the band, it's right under my boobs and it's like I have a pool noodle wrapped around my waist. The only thing that would cover up the bulge is a sweatshirt and I think that totally defeats the purpose of wearing shapewear.

How do I make it so I never have to sweep my floors again? Ooo, I know, dirt floors!

I could go on for a while with these questions, but I think I've made my point. For a long time, when I read magazines I felt like I was falling completely short when it came to society's views on how my home should look and smell. By the way, apparently it should always smell like some type of Verbena. I don't know what a verbena is, it might mean soap, because I see that word on small hotel soaps all the time. It could also be a flower, but honestly, I care so little about what it means, I'm not even going to look it up to verify my guess. Maybe I like the mystery.

At this point in my life, I don't want a pristine house anymore. I try to think about how much money I've saved on not buying magazines. They literally have nothing to say to me that I don't already know. I just want a house I can't wait to get home to, not to clean, but to laugh in, to cry in, to love in, to LIVE in. It's that simple.

# Make Someone Else Do it

Just because I didn't want to emulate magazines anymore, it didn't mean I was completely satisfied with the state of my home.

During a manic cleaning phase, spurred by the daintiest woman I've ever seen; I purged, I trashed, dumped, heaped, and banished many things from my house that no longer served a purpose. The "Magic" of cleaning and de-cluttering became a huge fad around that time. A woman from Japan who, in her book, talked fondly about cleaning up her family's mess when she was little spearheaded the movement. Not my ideal childhood experience, but hey, it worked for her.

I started with the clothes since I had so many items I never wore, and that's where the book told me to start. I took every type of clothing, shirts, pants, underwear, and even down to rogue single-socks, and I put them all on my bed. I sorted them into categories and, piece-by-piece, I decided what I should keep or get rid of. Most of it went in the trash, some went to donation bags, and I kept a decent number of things. The key, according to the tidying guru, was I had to touch and really look at each thing before I decided what to do with it. I made a lot of progress throughout the night, and then I got to the hard part.

On one shirt, I spent extra time holding and even smelling.

It was a dark, olive-green shirt. A swatch of pattern depicting a Japanese styled dragon with a forked tongue ran down the middle of it. Within the pattern, there were flames and camouflage. It was the type of shirt only Dungeons and Dragons players would own. This shirt was my dad's though, and I'm a thousand percent positive he never played D & D. Mom had given it to me, for posterity sake after he died.

A year prior to the big cleanout, I had gone through a similar bout of getting rid of things. I just couldn't get rid of the shirt back then. It was ugly, too big for me, and ridiculously cheesy. After cleaning out some things that first time, I had folded the shirt up and put it back in a drawer.

Now, I was faced with the decision of whether or not to get rid of the shirt again. But this shirt was dad's. I couldn't throw it away, I thought to myself.

Confession time. I'd always wanted to write a book, but lacked the motivation or discipline to put in the writing time. I only wrote when forced to in school and the occasional Facebook post. I thought it perfectly fine to walk around, considering myself a writer without writing a damn thing.

I don't know a lot about my dad's life prior to him being my father. All I knew about his past was he was born in Puerto Rico, was married once, and had two children with another woman who wasn't my mom. Then he moved to New York and worked as a jeweler for a Hasidic Jewish boss. He once lived in Ohio, and met my mom in Indiana.

At some point, my parents moved our family to New Jersey, then eventually back to Indiana.

Jump to 2011, and I decided I wanted to change jobs within the Army. I went to a school for journalism and became a military journalist. The school sparked my interest in writing again, plus it was a refresher in HOW to write. I eventually started writing for fun, and spent a whole day at the library, to learn how to set up a blog. Initially, writing had been this scary endeavor that I was sure no one would want to read. I worked my daytime job, but still desperately wanted to be a writer. I didn't know what to write. I also had the need to know who my dad was, so I started there.

I realized though, to discover who my dad was, I needed the mess of my surroundings to go. Often, I'd sit at my desk and feel the clutter around me pushing into my brain, and I couldn't write anything. I wanted life to run just a tad more smoothly before I could open up those throbbing closed wounds dad left in my chest.

That night, during my cleaning session, I looked at the pile of fabric littering my bed. I took a moment, sat down on top of it all, and held that awful shirt. For the life of me, I couldn't remember my dad ever wearing it.

I thought of him, and remembered a blue striped button down shirt and crisp but silky, gray slacks. He didn't wear pants, he wore slacks, in his healthy days. I say healthy in relative terms, as he was as healthy as a recovering alcoholic overeater can be. I also remembered a dark blue robe, no pants, just stained tighty-whities underneath. His belly and man boobs always stuck out of the opening because he never tied the sash right. I'm pretty sure he saw nothing wrong with wearing that tragedy, as he sat on the front porch looking at traffic go by, legs spread wide. Hey, that's what Puerto Ricans do...they look at traffic.

In my room, I touched the shirt to my face and felt...nothing.

That shirt wasn't my dad.

Getting rid of it wasn't getting rid of memories of him. I looked at that shirt and couldn't picture him in it. If I threw it away, all it meant was that I was getting rid of a shirt no one should be caught dead in. Instead, I chose to keep the thick cream scarf he had from the hospital. He didn't need it anymore, but I did.

I thanked the shirt for serving my dad as long as it did, and placed it into the donation bag, set to go off to someone else. Hopefully, they would find it at Goodwill, their eyes would widen and they'd wear it the very day they bought it, proudly strutting about town, looking like a pure badass.

Months later, I finished going through everything else. I went through each category of things that made up my life. I went through books, photos, kitchen stuff, paperwork, and other miscellaneous things. I got rid of about half of my worldly possessions.

I didn't know what to do with the stuff I kept, though.

The cleanup seemed easy enough. If a certain item wasn't beautiful or useful, I got rid of it. If it sparked my interest, it went into a temporary drawer space or corner of the dining room table.

I only had so many drawers to stuff things away in. The problem came when it was time to give all of the tiny and large things that made up my life a home. Where should that chip clip go? Where would be the best place for my DVD cleaner machine that I haven't quite decided if it was too stupid to keep?

It was time to call in a professional.

So, here's what happens when you call in a professional organizer to arrange your household. I Googled personal organizers in my area and pretty much went with the first legit website I found. Boyfriend agreed to hire her because he liked an article she wrote about the do's and don'ts of organizing your house. He specifically liked that she said not to touch your partner's things because it's a gross mistake to disturb their privacy and sense of self, they live there too after all.

The first step in the process would be to talk with "The Chosen One" over the phone to discuss concerns about my home. I mean really, the issue was I lived with someone else who didn't have the same idea of clean as I did. I don't remember her name, but we'll call her Andrea.

I've found with men, at least Boyfriend, if they can't see an item erotically displayed on their dresser or table, it doesn't exist. Never mind you've told them fifty times where the flashlight, with the 2.5-inch-diameter-lightbeam, is located. Just for the record, it never was, is not now, and will never be in the spot you tell them, because they've moved it since the last time it was used and you saw it with your own eyes.

I told Andrea, "He's a wonderful man and the only thing we ever fight about is 'stuff', but that stuff is enough to cause me to plot his accidental drowning." She then made me feel normal by describing her husband's quirks on organizing. She made me feel safe in letting her see my mess.

The next step was the first meeting at my home. I purposely didn't clean so she could properly assess the damage. She surprised me by saying I was mostly organized already, I just had to tuck in some bits.

It's slightly uncomfortable inviting a stranger into your home where she can look in all your nooks and crannies...luckily there were no stray underwear behind doors or in corners that day. She looked at all the rooms in the house, and I wrote a check for the initial meeting and a deposit for a shopping trip appointment later in the week. She would be my personal shopper. I was convinced she was going to take the check and I'd never see her again. I imagined myself, week after week, not cleaning a single room in the hopes she would show up.

I was relieved when she showed up to meet me at a local store where we'd agreed to do the shopping. She said first, we had to find a specific structure of, well, wood, I don't know what else to call it. It didn't have to be a cabinet per se, but I needed a shelf, stand or box specifically to house some things in my dining room. I decided that was the worst part of the house I wanted to work on the most. I was tired of the dining room table being a dumping ground from everything to purses, to mail, to everything else Boyfriend tracks in from the outside world.

We sat at tables in the grocery and household items store. The produce section had five tables, I don't know why. I guess people eat their lunches there, right in the grocery store, and it made me kind of depressed thinking of a businessman sitting at the crappy table, eating his chicken salad sandwich among the fruit section. I'd totally be tempted to steel kiwis if I ate there for lunch.

Andrea showed me a Pinterest page she had specifically designed with all my ideas and concerns in mind, and we hit the aisles. I bought a few odds and ends, as well as the 'signature' piece of furniture that would go in the dining room in order to keep all of the backpacks and my purses in one area.

Almost immediately I found what I was looking for. I guess that's the goal, to go in with a plan. Before, I had always just wandered stores not really having a plan and bought multiple baskets or trays, not sure where they would go once I brought them home.

The big difference this time was that I had a surefire idea of what I needed specifically to organize all the things, and having that plan made it go fast. We then hit up Target, where for the first time in the history of my life, I managed to spend less than $200 in a Target store.

We parted ways, and I went home to set everything up. Boyfriend even helped put together the organizer. Screw you Ikea, I can fight with Boyfriend for a lot cheaper when I shop local.

The result came fast. I had spent months trying to accomplish the task without success. But, with a professional as my guide, it only took about two hours at the most to finish the refined dining room setup. I placed everything in the divided stand and carefully set trays on top of it to separate all the tiny pieces. The heaviness in my chest subsided and I swear my wooden floors creaked a little less as I floated across them, admiring the emptiness where clutter and mess used to be.

I had a few areas left that I wasn't sure what to do with, so Andrea visited one more time to check out the progress and helped more with the bookcases and the other things still in the dining room. She dove right in with lots of energy and it was fun seeing how excited she was as things came together.

The greatest thing about the experience was even though I had someone helping me, it all came down to what I thought looked good and felt right. The lack of 'stuff' cluttering my home allowed me to start to clear out some of the mental clutter I had. I faced the memories I feared, memories I never had time to banish, because I was too busy tidying. That clarity allowed me to write about dad's death, as well as search for more about his life and my own. The process was more than trying to put physical things in order. It freed up time to sit and be with what I had.

# Things People Tell You When You're Fat

It's a story as old as time. Teenage girl needs to get ready for school, emotional breakdown ensues. The girl sits by the closet, clothes strewn everywhere. She puts on a shirt, runs to the bathroom mirror, looks at herself and proceeds to rip it off and rushes back to the closet to find the other shirt she tried on three times ago.

A morning like most others, mom yelled up the stairs, "You're going to be late, you better get down here soon." Look, I wish it didn't sound like such a scripted phrase in every single tween movie set in the last decade, but that's what moms say, verbatim, in every household in America.

"I can't!" I screamed at her. "I've already worn everything I own this week. If I wear the same thing again, everyone will make fun of me, and they'll know we're poor. If they know I'm poor, the boys will know I don't have a dowry, and then I'll never get married. And when it's time for me to die alone, the Diablo de Fashion will arise, and he will drag me to hell, where I'll be stuck in a loop for eternity, matching socks fresh out of the dryers of the abyss and they're black socks with slightly varying seam patterns."

This was how the whole "getting dressed" scenario usually worked out for me. Usually, the only other things in my 13-year-old world that caused such distress were science classes. These teenage stressors threw me into fits of wailing and thrashing. I had a keen knack for summoning a Linda Blair level of craziness in either situation.

I'd like to imagine all young girls reacted this way to picking out clothes, but I'm not sure. I feel like every female on the planet, at some point in their life, has had issues with self-esteem and their bodies. Save those anomalies who came out of the womb fabulous and confident. I, however felt like a huge whale most of my adolescence, only wales did way more swimming than me as I could never find a bathing suit that was practical as well as wasn't just an oversized wet suit.

The main problem with me was, the thoughts of myself as fat and overweight had been validated while I was growing up.

Around my house, my family regularly referred to me as "the human garbage disposal." They weren't exactly wrong, if there was food left over on someone else's plate, it was going in my mouth. I wore a size 16/18 when I was twelve. Mind you, I'm only 4' 10" now, which probably would have put me at about, oh four total feet back then. I was pretty stout and roundish. This fact alone isn't a bad thing, people are people at all sizes and they love, and slay, and explode in laughter all the same. We all deserve to feel good about ourselves regardless. Unfortunately, schools are rarely a good place to be that size and build confidence at the same time.

At night, I'd binge on olives, crackers with cream cheese, then decide at 2am that deviled eggs were sounding like a viable dessert.

I received my fair share of bullying because of my weight. Boys yelled I needed to get on a stair stepper and they told me to my face that I was disgusting. I once had the courage to have my friend Anna ask a boy out for me. She took a while getting back to me, but finally laid it out.

"He said he likes you and you're funny, but you're too fat," said Anna. This would become a regular occurrence. I eventually became the go-between from boys I liked who only used me to give messages to my friends that were considered hot.

But Mike, good old Mike, he took it to another level, basically torturing me during middle school. I wore a dress one day and thought I looked rather lovely. It was black with big yellow and orange plastic flowers on it and probably a little shorter than I should have dared, according to Mike. I loved it though. He sat behind me in math class and continuously whispered in my ear that I looked awful. Now that I think of it, this was ironic, because he was by no means thin.

"Your freckles are so ugly," said Mike. I sat there silent, staring forward. "Hey piggy piggy, I'm talking to you," he said a little louder, so others sitting around us could hear. "Why are you so fat? Answer me piggy?" This went on for a few minutes, but I continued to ignore him.

When I started to well up with tears, I heard another deep and loud voice.

"You should probably shut the fuck up before I get out of my chair and beat your ass," someone said. Jerome was my knight in baggy pants and huge hair, and he came to my rescue.

Mike stuttered a little and sat back in his chair. He didn't say a single word to me during the rest of the class.

It chokes me up to think about that day. Jerome really had no reason to stick up for me. We weren't friends and I'm pretty sure we never had a conversation before that day. Despite the violent connotations of his statement, it was the kindest thing anyone had ever done for me. I don't think Jerome will ever know how much the act of standing up for me, for nothing in return, helped me.

Mike didn't stop taunting me outside of class, though. One day he came up to me in the lunchroom as I sat eating my food.

"Hey fatty, you should stop eating, you're going to break the chair," Mike said. A strange feeling came over me. I wasn't sad. I wasn't embarrassed, or afraid, I was angry. I was a motherfucking Bonano, and I immediately thought about the idea that I would CUT a bitch. Generally, I was a peaceful person, likely to cry at everything. To this day, I cry sometimes just looking at how beautiful my cat is. I was not ever going to cut anything on that boy, but I did feel like I could do something to make it all stop.

I lurched up from the table, my chair went flying behind me and I took a step towards Mike. I knifed my hand and put it an inch from his nose. I had never hit anyone before so my punching reflex wasn't quite up to par. I didn't say a word. Sweat ran down his face as I stared into his beady little eyes.

"Ok, ok, I was just playing, hey we're cool right?" he asked. I refused to speak to him and he turned on his heel and walked away, never to open his flappy mouth again.

I'm not sure that would have happened without the push from Jerome. His words let me know that it wasn't ok for someone to treat me that way.

As an official grownup, I stand in my closet now and I don't sob over how I have nothing to wear.

I have more workout clothes and sweatpants than "going out" clothes and that's perfectly acceptable to me. My weight fluctuation makes sweatpants a must, and stretch denim is a gift from the gods. It took me even longer to become legitimately comfortable in my body.

The blow to my self-image cut deep in college. There was no way to compete with the striking women on campus. They were corn fed but somehow still thin, tanned goddesses with brilliant hair. I inevitably quit trying to look presentable. I wore pajama pants to most of my classes and my hair was usually in a bun.

You know what bad thing happened?

Not one bad thing happened. No one made fun of me. Not one person told me to my face that I was a slob. Not to brag here, but, fun fact, even though I was considered overweight by society's standards, and there were so many gorgeous women on campus, I still got laid, like a lot.

Years later, things took another turn towards the depressing. Even though I had Boyfriend, I began to feel gross and unattractive, because yet again, I'd gained weight.

I walked with my head down and I never looked at anyone when I passed by. I didn't give two shits about what I looked like at work. When I first started at the police department, the dress code was business casual. I put in a lot of effort to look crisp, flashy, and delicate. After about two years, I did what I had to, just enough, to fall in line with the dress code. An amazing thing I discovered was that if I ordered a shirt that had the department's logo on it, I could get any type of shirt I wanted out of a catalogue. My beautiful, wonderful sweatshirts were back in my life and I could wear them at work.

I thought my feelings of inadequacy were a symptom of my body looking the way it did. I tried to make my body into something that would remedy those feelings. I worked out, but not nearly as much as I should have. Honestly, I ate like shit. Fried food was my lifeline, and fast food was my confidant and mood stabilizer. Weekday beer binges didn't do me any favors either. I wished I could be the kind of girl who likes clear alcohol, because as all my magazines told me, they have fewer calories. I just couldn't be that girl though, the one who loves shooters, or Rum splashed with Diet Coke, and forget straight vodka. I don't like beverages that literally hurt my throat. Therefore, I always defaulted to beer. There's no telling what I'd look like if I didn't drink beer, and unfortunately, I'm not at a juncture in time to find out. Maybe one day I'll quit drinking, just not today.

I was constantly surprised that Boyfriend still wanted to have sex with me. When I look back at it though, it was usually in the dark and lasted just long enough to classify it as a notch on the bedpost. Many mornings he'd tell me I'd feel better if I went to CrossFit with him. Um, also, if anyone ever tells you that, call him or her a fucking liar.

You will not feel better after CrossFit. Yeah, you'll feel ok about the fact that you did a numbingly hard work out, but the next day you'll feel like you have bone cancer as everything hurts and your legs and arms don't work the way they're supposed to.

I tried to be the good girlfriend and went with him for about two years. Whenever I regularly attended classes, I felt broken. Prior to the workouts, I'd feel nauseous and scared because I knew I would be miserable during the WOD (workout of the day). Every day before class, I had to take an emergency poo because I was so nervous. During the workouts, I prayed that I'd break my leg so I could stop, because many of the exercises burned every fiber of my body and made me want to pee in my fancy leggings I bought just for CrossFit. After the classes, I couldn't lift my legs to put on clean underwear. So yeah, Boyfriend was lying when he said I would feel better. He just wanted me to get off the couch. He never outright said I had gained too much weight, but I knew it bothered him.

In his own way he loved me, but my feelings about my weight and the overall depression made it so I wasn't even me anymore, and I guess that was something he could never tell me. "I love you, but I'm not in love with you anymore."

# You Don't Have to Put a Ring on it

It's interesting to me how strangers are more concerned with my reproductive health and marriage status than I am. I was at my yearly appointment with the vagina doctor a couple years ago and Dr. Connerly insisted on conversation while his face was in my crotch.

"Yep, you've got a lovely and healthy uterus," he said, holding his flashlight in his mouth. Ok, it probably wasn't in his mouth and I don't know if there was even a flashlight, but either way, it's always an awkward situation to be in. Dr. Connerly was an older gentleman and he reminded me of a grandpa, sweet as pie; which I'm not really sure what that says about me, that I'd rather have an old guy do medical things to my lady parts, rather than a woman or hot Dr. McSteamy. Side note, to this day I resent that a doctor was the first male to ever touch my boobs.

"Thanks, I guess," I replied. I was strangely proud of my womb. No one had ever told me about the merits of my vulva and uterus before, and I smiled to myself. "I have to ask, are you taking any prenatal vitamins?" he asked.

I told him no, and he said that was ok. It was just, if I were thinking about having kids, I should really consider taking prenatal vitamins, and do some reading up on what I could do for my fertility health. You know, just so my body would be ready when I was to procreate. Well, being that I was there for birth control, no, no I wasn't thinking about having kids anytime soon. In fact, I was thinking about having my tubes tied while he was down there. I was 27 at the time.

I get mixed results when I tell people I don't think I'm going to have children. This isn't a new phenomenon; women choosing not to become mothers, so I think people are less opinionated than they used to be.

Sometimes people tell me it's perfectly normal to not want to be a mom, not everyone is doing it these days. Others tell me I'll change my mind eventually, it's the hardest job I'll ever have, but it will totally be worth it. When they do, I think it's nice that someone else can know what I want out of life, because I sure as hell don't. They never say it while looking me in the eyes.

I can't trust my inebriated self when it comes to major life decisions. After one date night, I stumbled into the house ahead of Boyfriend. I left one item of clothing per square foot of space throughout the house, leading to the bathroom. He came inside to find me sitting on the toilet and guided me upstairs as I crawled to the bedroom. I mumbled to him that I wanted to make a baby, while sloppily kissing at his face. He kindly pushed it away, and I eventually went to sleep. The next morning, I woke up and looked at my makeup-smeared face in the mirror. I felt thankful that I didn't have to take care of a baby with my pounding headache.

I can't imagine a little being looking at me and asking me what it's supposed to do. I have enough trouble looking after my pets and myself. I can't find my phone right now as I type. I'm terrible at self-censorship and would probably call the kid an asshole to its face at least once. I'd hate myself when they'd turn to heroin because I never even pretended Santa Claus was real.

I certainly won't know what to do if I had a little girl.

"Mom, Tommy was so mean to me at school today. He's so cute and I love him, why did he call me fat?" she would ask.

I would kneel in front of her and look at her sweet face. "It's because Tommy's a dick and doesn't like you, Matilda," I would say. "People will tell you he's mean and he teases you because he likes you. They'll even tell you he hit you because he likes you. That's bullshit, Matilda. People don't hit someone they love. Next week, he'll tell you you're pretty and try to put his hands down your pants. And when you go off to college, he'll visit you once, you'll have sex in your dorm room, and he will tell you he loves you, even though he just had sex with Becky three days ago and didn't tell you. Even if you two were to get married one day and live happily ever after, it won't really be happily ever after; you're going to have to wash his dirty underwear, feed him, and he'll buy you a knife set for Valentine's Day. That is if he gets you anything. And you're going to have to nag him every single day for the rest of your life to take the garbage out. And when you turn 40, he's going to fall in love with Sharon in Human Resources with the big teeth. She understands him and you never gave him the attention he needed. Then, he's going to leave you, run your credit card to the max, and disappear to Fiji."

Then, my daughter will blink her beautiful brown eyes and cry. Nope, not something I think I'm prepared to deal with.

I also avoid weddings because again, strangers like to ask me questions that are none of their fucking business, like when I'm getting married. If you're over the age of 13 and ask a single woman this question, you should be ashamed and go take a shot of go fuck yourself. It's like saying to them, "Why are you incompetent at being a woman and failing at life?"

Seriously, that's what you're implying when you ask a wonderful, living, beautiful woman, why no one has made her theirs, and announced it in the papers. There is no good answer we could give these people who ask such silly questions. I swear, I could win a Pulitzer and all that people would ask me at weddings is when I'm getting hitched, implying I'm doing the whole relationship thing wrong. I've made it a point the next time someone asks this, I'm going to reply with, "Because I don't give enough blow jobs." I'll call it a day and fist pump all the way to the dance floor, where I'll dance with Uncle Bob, and maybe let him see my boobs. There's always an Uncle Bob at those things.

It's a shame though, because I do love weddings. It's a reason to dress up and look way hotter than I do on any other night, formal wear just gets me, man.

I've never been jealous of all my friends when they get married (I might be lying here…ok, sometimes I am jealous). My favorite part of the ceremony is when everyone stands up because they start playing the "entrance song," whichever corny one they pick, and I turn and the shining bride walks down the aisle. I tear up every time and try not to look at Boyfriend because I don't want to make him feel like a trapped animal, waiting for the slaughter.

I also adore the kiss, it's always weird and contrived, and their mouths never touch at the right angle, but it's still beautiful in a not-Hollywood, gross kind of way. Then I proceed to imagine setting everyone else on fire because they have their phones out, taking pictures, as if they could take a better one than the photographer getting paid to take pictures.

I hate the reception, I love the cake, but hate the chicken dance.

The problem with the reception is that normal married people get wasted at the open bar, argue, and grope their spouses because they haven't been outside their homes without their children in five years. Then these assholes come and sit down next to Boyfriend and me. There's not much worse than trying to make small talk with people you don't know.

"So, how long have you guys been together?" Wifey asks, her eyes glazed and she's teetering her head as she rests it on her fist. She stares at me, with her big dumb wedding ring glaring in the chandelier light, hurting my eyes. Honestly, I'm not bitter at all.

"Almost eight years, how about you guys, how long have you been married?" I ask Wifey.

Husband chimes in, "We've been together three long years, married one," he says and continues with, "Oh jeez, eight years huh? Well, when are you two getting married, you're not getting any younger." He is probably also thinking I should have a baby soon, otherwise the kid could have chromosomal problems, like that would be a horrible thing, it wouldn't. I would love that unwanted baby regardless.

I look at Boyfriend with the why-aren't-we-married look, and shrug my shoulders. Boyfriend usually stammers, and I don't listen to his reply. What I really want to say to these people is, "Because I still fuck him with abandon, make him pancakes without any paperwork on file, and he's waiting until I don't anymore so he can walk away with minimal fees. Please, tell me, when was the last time you two had sex?"

The couple would look at me, then each other, and get up to leave the table. Then I will high five Boyfriend and show him my boobs.

I've read that you can tell the success and love level of a couple by listening to them recite the story of how they met. I've watched Boyfriend retell the tale numerous times. He never gets any less excited than the first time he's ever told it, "And then, I just grabbed her bag and carried it to the helicopter." He barely contains himself when he recalls another of "our" stories. He says, "Not everyone can say they've held hands with the person they love on an Army helicopter," no my man, they all certainly can't.

I don't know if Boyfriend will ever ask me to marry him. I don't even know if I want him to, or what I would answer. I do know, eight years after kissing him for the first time, I still want to kiss him. I also still want to grab his butt. For now, that is enough. (Post Script, Boyfriend did not in fact ask me to marry him, and two years later, we have both moved on.)

He would make beautiful babies though. (Also…I lied, he would NOT make cute babies).

# Please Clear My History

One rainy day, I was crossing a busy downtown street. Even though the light was red, the oncoming vehicle didn't think it should stop first, before turning right. I also didn't think I needed to stop walking through the crosswalk either because I had the right of way, granted, I didn't have the WALK sign. We were both kind of right and kind of wrong. Probably I was wrong though.

I don't think I could have been held accountable though, had I been hit, because it was raining ya'll. I was soaked and on a mission to get back to the office from a bank trip, that was more like a journey to Mordor. I had slammed my hand on the bank door and was bleeding. By Gandalf though, I dropped that bank deposit into the depths of what is also known as Wells Fargo.

The odd part of almost dying (I'm being ridiculously dramatic here) was what I thought as the car screeched to a halt, coming closer than I'd ever like to admit to hitting me. My life didn't flash before my eyes, I didn't think about what kind of underwear I had on, trust me, it didn't matter anyways. No, I thought, "Fuck, someone's going to see my YouTube history and they're going to tell everyone not to come to the funeral, because I was THAT weird."

I joined the YouTube train car a little late in the game, but trust me, I've been making up for lost time.

It started innocent enough. Initially, I searched Newsreel bloopers, where a newscaster was trying to record a segment and some random person in the background would pull out their penis. I transitioned into using the videos to feed emotions I wanted to feel. I invited myself to cry by watching service member homecomings and dog videos. I watched calming videos to help me fall asleep at night.

I even relearned how to set a mousetrap. One day, I knew how to set one, the next I didn't, and the video was very informative and thankfully didn't show a mouse get murdered in an unaware blissful state of licking peanut butter off the trap. Sometimes I feel guilty about being a mouse serial killer, but I mean, we could totally get along if they just didn't shit on my counters. It's like they eventually started doing it out of spite. The mice got hip to the fact that I was trying to kill them and stopped eating off the traps. They'd leave little mouse turds completely all around the contraption, where I'd find it in the morning and scream obscenities, but secretly, I was relieved I didn't have to dispose of another body.

When I deployed to Afghanistan for the second time, my YouTube viewings got a little desperate. Straight Rom Com levels of pathetic questions and goals.

I had been with Boyfriend for eight years, and let's just say, I let myself go. As it often tends to do, the lusty wantings and craziness of the relationship were waning. Add in the long distance (Me in Afghanistan, him in Indiana), I wasn't feeling connected to him. I wore a uniform every day and I felt frumpy.

I decided to quit wallowing in self-pity and got down to working on myself, I know, that's a first right, a 30 something woman working on herself? Relationships have the same rules, I didn't want to sit around, waiting for our partnership to degrade more. I turned to YouTube instead of body oil and candles to relight the spark. I searched, 'How to tell if your boyfriend likes you,' or the always original, 'how to please your man,' followed by tutorials from fancy looking women on how to be feminine, or 'how to be a lady.' The thing that bothered me was, none of the advice included wearing mu mu's, and I found that very disappointing. I searched, 'how to be sexy,' but that one usually just brought up a lot of videos making fun of women trying to be sexy. Most of the clips told me to be myself, and there's nothing sexier than a confident woman. No shit Jeeves, you're telling me I just gotta' be confident with what I got going on already and it'll all be ok?

I tried to refine the search, but vague tips on going out into the world and rocking it were of no help. So, I tried to break down what 'sexy' would mean to me.

I looked for videos on how to dress a short body that was only slightly pudgy. Back home, before the deployment, I had gotten into a habit of wearing sweatshirts and cargo pants every day. Basically, all the videos said it came down to wearing maternity shirts to flatter my body. Ok, that's not entirely true, but that was what it felt like. The videos suggested wearing shirts with empire waists and cinching cardigans with belts. This doesn't work for me because I find belts completely cumbersome, it takes me long enough to go to the bathroom.

I looked up videos shouting at me that I'm awesome! They said I should just accept that and continue to be awesome and, again, this came up over and over, to be myself, because that's the best way to be attractive. Really, I thought it was being a size four, with shiny hair, and six-foot long legs. But who am I to question the rules?

"Oh, but what about that plus sized model Ashley Graham, she's not skinny and she's a model?" I've heard people point out in the skinny vs. curvy debate. Well, as you mention it, she also has a gorgeous face that doesn't fit society's view of what a 'fat face' looks like and is often seen as unattractive. She is not a size two, but her proportions are that of an hourglass, something always coveted by men and women. She is a gorgeous fucking woman, point blank, Photoshop or not.

"Oh no!" the videos say, you don't have to be gorgeous; just be happy, smile, and everyone will like you. Then, you can have any guy you want, have your own hobbies, your own life, and they'll come crawling. Or, your current manfriend will fall in love with you all over again. Uh, Mr. Internet, what if my hobbies are reading self-help books and drinking beer while doing laundry? Boyfriend isn't exactly turned on by my habit of spouting, "Not tonight honey, I've got to finish this chapter in Harry Potter, maybe after."

Look guys, I don't have body dimorphic disorder. I know what I look like and I consider my self-image as realistic. I wasn't ok with that for a long time, but things got better. In the past, I tolerated how I felt about myself. Now, I'm damn fond of the smorgasbord of sometimes great hair, and sometimes a bloaty tummy I'm working with.

More online research involved me looking for ways to connect with my yoni (sounds like Toney, and it means 'vagina' according to one sexual guru woman on YouTube). Adina, the goddess on the screen, had a whole channel about; feeling your best, sex, and relationship tips. The video about vagina health was traumatizing. She used the P word like it was no big deal, like she was saying the word antelope. The concept of just blurting out pussy in everyday conversations was foreign.

Another vajayjay tip was to peel a cucumber and….you know…put it on up there because it's good for cleaning your cooter out, kills bacteria, and it's very cooling and whatnot. I mean, mine isn't on fire generally speaking so I don't even know what that's about.

Adina also told me to talk to my vagina. This is how that conversation went:

Me: "Hey, Cecilia (that's her name), what's up?"
Vagina: …..
Me: "Come on, don't be like that, talk to me."
Vagina: "I don't have anything to say, I just want to be left alone except for approximately one day out of the year, why are you doing this?"
Me: "I just want to know how you're feeling."
Vagina: "Clammy."
Me: "Forget it," stomps off and eats Oreos, even though the video said to eat citrus fruits because that would make

Cecilia more appealing to sniff because that's always a concern.

The video on vagina health was plain entertaining. I did think the idea of giving my hooha some sunshine with a sunbath was pleasant sounding, though I'm not really sure how legally I could make that work out. I may revisit the video one day, but not today. I do plan on drinking more water though, that's the fix for everything.

The night I discovered makeup tutorial videos turned out to be a five-hour exercise in futility.

You mean I can put makeup on to look ten pounds lighter without running seven miles today? Sign me right the fuck up.

I watched hours of instruction on how to make my pores look smaller, and how to use contour powder to sculpt cheekbones that can cut hard cheeses. Mostly, it felt like I had the skill level of a toddler trying to improve the Mona Lisa with finger-paints. I put the contour powder on and it just looked like I was smudging dirty soot on my cheeks. The videos promised I could make my hooded eyes into a completely different shape. I ended up looking like Alice Cooper on a bender, out in the rain.

A lot of money was spent on Amazon ordering makeup and special brushes, in a "war zone," while deployed to Afghanistan. This made me feel guilty for a whole slew of reasons. Back home, everyone assumed I was in rough conditions, living in a tent. That tour, I had it pretty good. I had my own room, I wasn't eating prepackaged Soldier meals, and bad guys weren't trying to kill me, for the most part. I felt bad, until I remembered, hey, I did live in a tent in Iraq. I did have to pee out in the middle of nowhere while out on mission, I had gone hungry because cold food just wasn't worth it back then, and I'd had my crotch grabbed by a local national who was supposed to be getting water out of my vehicle.

I'd earned this break.

I kept watching the makeup videos at night and kept trying. Soon, I could make my eyes look sultry. I didn't wear a full face of makeup at work, because that would just be silly. I could, however, do my makeup in the privacy of my own room and just look at myself. Not half bad, I thought.

Back in the states, I usually only looked in the mirror long enough to see my shirt wasn't on backwards before I headed off to my civilian job. I wouldn't say I avoided mirrors at home, I just didn't hang out with them very much.

In Afghanistan though, I had a mirror on the back of my door, in a very tiny room. Every morning, I'd wake up to stare at my crazy hair and remember it was ok, because I'd just put it in a bun. I'd get undressed from my sleeping clothes, usually sweats, and see myself naked. On the deployment, I lost some weight, enough for my back fat to disappear. I'd often stand in front of the mirror, looking at my body from different angles as it changed from day to day. I eventually stopped looking away.

I think a lot of times, people can't find beauty in things that are foreign to them. For most of my life, that's what my body was. It was foreign and I never really saw it. It was there, doing what it had to, to get through each day. It was simply a workhorse.

As each day went on, I started to see my body. I looked closer at it in the mirror. The lines of my collarbone were quite pretty. The outline of my hips didn't seem so gargantuan anymore, they were curvy and plentiful. My curly hair started to look like "bed head" in a good way. The curve of my belly still looked as soft as ever, but this was no longer a bad thing. My legs though, oh my legs. My thighs were round, but when I looked down toward where the thigh muscles met the knees, they looked strong, like dancer's legs, maybe not quite ballerina-esq, more like a Cha Cha Slide queen. Still, a dancer's legs they were. My ankles, like my wrists, were dainty. Shit guys, maybe even feminine, dare I say.

My face still felt fatter than the subject of a Botero painting sometimes. But now, I can just slap some magic cream on, blend away, and I'm Kate Moss for a day. Not really, I'm not THAT good, nor would I want to be. Even if I don't have time, or the desire to put makeup on, I can still look at myself as a whole and it's pretty damn sensational (depending on the day you ask me). As I've aged, I like what I see more and more and I can't wait until I'm 80 and even more in love with what I see. Finger's crossed.

# Bathroom Blues

One thing I know for sure is that in any military setting, using the bathroom is pretty much not going to be enjoyable. There are only a few scenarios you're going to encounter.

Porta Potties are aplenty. They are the plastic miniature houses for doing the business when regular bathrooms aren't practical, which is in every Army situation. The blue water splashes up on your butt when something drops too fast and too furious. Sometimes though, you can read pure poetry about Chuck Norris on the dank walls.

Once, I opened the door to a Porta Potty and it looked like someone had taken a tampon by it's string and spun it around like helicopter propellers, either that or someone died, I don't know. Your guess is as good as mine. Lots of times though, people just forego pooping inside the actual bowl and just go on the floor. Yep, I've stepped in human poop before.

Other times in the military, the bathrooms are trailers that usually overflow. It's kind of a game, I think, to see how much shit one can get in the toilet before it backs up.

At times, I had to go to the bathroom in a facility with no stalls at all, just a bunch of toilet bowls lined up in a row. The first time I ever used that kind of bathroom I was mortified. What do you mean I must pee with someone sitting right next to me? Eventually, I got used to it and now, I like to lock eyes with people right as I'm going. I imagine it's how my dog feels when I watch him.

Worst-case scenario, there are no bathroom facilities.

Like with any other crappy ( he he ) situation, I've found it's pretty important to adapt in order to keep some semblance of humor. I do this by imagining my dream bathroom. It's so big, you could host Thanksgiving dinner for 10 in it, and it's so clean Martha Stewart would go there, to just, hang out. It has heated floors and an unlimited supply of toilet paper. I imagine it smells like underwear model pheromones with a splash of incense, and I couldn't forget the verbena.

In 2011, I was attached to a Marine unit as a public affairs specialist in Helmand Province, Afghanistan. This meant I was a journalist for the Army.

It wasn't a particularly dangerous gig, as my commander usually wouldn't let us go off base, therefore I took a lot of photos of cakes, and once wrote a story about a fire drill. A few times, I could go off base with another unit. That day, it was to be a simple patrol, followed by a meeting with elders of the area. We had to sit in our trucks for a few hours, waiting for the meet up time. We visited a few houses and gave a kid an energy drink, I'm not sure if it was a good thing or a bad thing. As soon as his fingers touched the tiny little can of pure sugar with a splash of whoopass ingredients, he held it above his head and let out a little shriek as if he'd just found the Holy Grail. Then, he took off running, pouring the liquid into his mouth.

Inevitably, the thing happened that always happens when I'm in a position where there are no bathrooms around. I had to pee.

I continued to sit in the truck, ate pop tarts, watched camels fight, and tried to hold my pee for as long as possible. Eventually, two of the Marines stepped out of the vehicle to do their business so I figured that was as good a time as any to go too. It was in the middle of nowhere. There were only a few mud hut houses in the distance, and farmers tending poppy fields, but mostly it was just flatness and sand.

I turned away from the Marines as they peed, I mean I like wangs and all, but I'm not a pervert. After they finished, I sidled myself slightly up under the vehicle, between the huge tires that were almost as tall as me. The sun beat down on me and I thought, "Oh well, vaj, smaj," I didn't care if anyone saw.

Luckily, once the two Marines were done going, they offered to pull security, facing away from me.

"Holy shit," I thought to myself. I had my own personal armed guards watching over me while I pissed in the desert. Take that Taliban. This was pre-ISIS.

I squatted and let loose. I sighed a breath of relief, holding my pants as far away from the stream as possible. A thousand squats couldn't have prepared me for how long I was going to be in that position. This was the piss of all pisses. There was radio traffic here and there, nothing really going on as I went for roughly three minutes straight, legs shaking. The pen in my shirt pocket fell out and landed between my feet. "Welp, that's a field loss," I told myself, as I got urine all over the pen.

Mid-stream, I heard over the radio we needed to get back in our trucks right then, at that exact moment. The situation had changed to where it wasn't safe to be outside of our vehicle anymore.

"Come on let's go, slice it off," one of the Marines said.

"But I can't stop," I said desperately.

I clenched my teeth and willed my bladder to hold the fuck on. Finally, I managed to stop peeing and yanked my pants up, not even bothering to tuck my shirt in because my vest was in the way, all the while terrified this would be how I was remembered if the terrorists decided to blow us up at that moment, footage of me with my pants down around my ankles all up on the interwebs.

I climbed back in the truck and waited for further guidance and the second Marine got in and turned to me. He was holding my pen up to my face.

"You dropped this," he said.

"Yew, thanks, I don't want it," I said shaking my head. I then watched him put it in his own pocket. Hopefully he didn't have the habit of chewing on pens. I didn't have the lady balls to tell him I'd peed on it. Since then, my personal record for consecutive waking hours of holding my urine is twelve agonizing hours. Compared to bathrooms in the military, my toilet at home is a shining beacon of laser light that symbolizes freedom. Freedom, I tell you.

When I'm ticked about peeing down the side of a mountain, or I've pissed all over my boots because I didn't angle right, I just think to myself, "Soon, soon I will be able to walk five feet from my bedroom to my bathroom. Soon I'll be home."

I will shuffle in the middle of the night, in the dark, to the commode and be back in my bed before I fully wake up. I shall wear no pants, no shoes, and it will be glorious. Have you noticed how important having no pants on is to me yet?

I think I'm one of the lucky ones though. My bathroom schedule was the biggest of my worries when it came to deployments, and for that I'm thankful. I'm not going to lie, I have Googled the possibility of getting a bladder transplant because I simply don't trust those nifty gadgets that allow a female to pee standing up.

# Home

I had been in Afghanistan for five months, on my second time there, third deployment overall. For the first time, I was sincerely missing home. It's surprising what spurred my feelings to the point I had to acknowledge them.

My workday was over and it was almost time to go back to my living quarters. Normally, I would drop my book bag onto my bed, then walk to the chow hall to get dinner in a Styrofoam to-go box, and bring it back so I could watch an hour of television while eating in a fold out chair. This isn't so bad because I lived with my two best friends. We usually talked like girls at a sleepover and bellowed with laughter until we collapsed at night into our beds.

Marie was one of the main reasons I went on that deployment in the first place. She was living in Illinois and I was in Indiana. She called me up one day and asked if I'd come to Afghanistan with her. Her unit needed another sergeant and I fit the bill. For six months, I drove six hours to where the unit was in preparation for the deployment. It went pretty much like the last two mobilizations, but this one was better because Marie was there.

It's no Matlock mystery most people choose to spend their time with those, who at the most, they love, and at the least, they can tolerate. I found under most dire challenges, having someone there who cares about you makes it all possible. To foster these relationships with others, when it comes time to pick friends, I'll look at a person and ask myself the following questions:

- Do they like caramel gelato as much as I do?
- Will they under most circumstances let me run in front of them as they go at a slower pace so the bears get them first?
- Is their ideal partner type opposite of what I go for?
- Do they have a truck?
- Will they let me wash my underwear with their clothes in the same washing machine?
- Will they share food and drink with me without worrying about spit?
- Most importantly: Will they turn a crappy situation into a good one, simply because they're there?

Marie pretty much met all or most of the requirements. I met her in 2007 during my first deployment. The first day we ever had an actual conversation, I forked over $300 bucks so she could buy a digital camera; taking her word she would pay me back.

She paid me back in full, with friendship interest.

The Army is like that when it comes to making friends. Often, I'll find myself standing next to a stranger in a line, waiting. I'm not waiting for anything particular, just waiting because I saw a line and figured I better get in it, and the next thing I know, I'm giving my waiting-buddy throat punches, because that's what friends do, and we just became friends.

On one of my few days off in Iraq, I planned on sleeping in, when to high and holy hell, I was startled awake by Marie's face right next to mine and she was shaking my arm. I was on the top bunk, because it totally makes sense to put the shortest person in the Army ever, on the top bunk.

I opened my eyes and said, "WHAT...what time is it?"

"Hey, I'm going to Dominoes to get some food, you want to come? She asked. "It's nine." Yes, it was that kind of deployment. We had Dominos, but we also had detainees that threw human shit at us, so it was the least the Army could do for us after fighting their war.

I stared at her for a good 30 seconds, trying to focus my eyes. Then I instantly became enraged.

"You must be out your godtdamnt mind!" I yelled at her. "NO, no, just no, I'm going back to sleep." I violently turned my body away from her. There she stood though, looking at me. Another 30 seconds went by in silence and I looked over my shoulder at her.

Then I whispered, "Will you get me a sandwich?"

I ended up getting dressed and going with her to get food.

This seems like a dumb example of friendship. I could've talked about being with her when the base was hit with IDF's, or when I was with her the night she found out she was going to be a mom, or the night my grandma died, when she drove to my house to scrape my wrecked and beer soaked body from the floor, and she put me to bed.

The Dominoes story, though, cements our friendship in my mind. For me, to get out of bed when I don't have to, man that's true love. I was far meaner to Boyfriend when he woke me up.

When the rain is pouring, and I'm cold, numb, and hungry; when I'm marching and I'm sure I cannot put my foot one more step ahead, I've felt someone pushing and shoving me from behind, shouldering my weight up the hill. Sure, I'm a fabulous and independent woman, but I'm not dumb enough to think I can do all things on my own.

I would choose to go even hungrier, more tired, and colder, if it meant I wouldn't be alone.

My very last deployment to Afghanistan, in 2015, hadn't been bad. I was safe and didn't work too hard by any means. One night though, I felt it, I felt incomplete. As I got ready to leave work, a flight was processing. My unit was basically TSA, but in Afghanistan. We checked all the outgoing personnel and their baggage to make sure they didn't have unauthorized weapons, rocks, or dildos. There was a military working dog on one flight. It was an all-black German Shepard, wearing the cutest miniature military vest you've ever seen. I initially thought seeing the pup would make me happy because I got to see a dog. It did the exact opposite. That dog wasn't mine, I hadn't raised it and it didn't love me.

Instantly, my heart squeezed shut and I thought about Dozer and Junior, my furry boys back at home. At the gate, the dog's handler said I could take pictures with the dog because I had a camera in my hand, for a completely unrelated project, but I didn't even want to. I left the office and went to my room. I dropped my book bag on my bed and tried not to cry. I just wanted to feel Dozer's fur between my fingers. I wanted to feel his fat ass next to me in bed. I wanted to spoon him and wake up to his kisses and pawing. I wanted to cook bacon in the kitchen with him sitting on the cold floor, waiting for bites as his drool puddled on the floor.

Couple this feeling of loss, with the fact that Boyfriend and I had some heavy conversations in those weeks and we weren't doing very well. I was simply tired, tired of wanting things I couldn't have. I was even angrier because I had chosen it all.

Friends are amazing, wonderful, and irreplaceable. But they can only fill in your cracks and holes so much when you're away from a partner. There's no way around it. Friends can't hug you the way Boyfriend can, nor can they kiss you on the forehead and have it feel as good.

At least that's what I thought for the longest time. I realized this wasn't true the day Marie decided she'd had enough of me and I was too tired to fight for her anymore. We ended our friendship a year later, but I'm convinced a kiss on my forehead from her now would feel a thousand times better than Boyfriend's pecks.

Monkeys who are raised without other monkey contact, actual physical contact, have been known to wither and die, even though all their other needs are met. I think humans are the same way. It's just not natural to not feel the skin of someone else and have it mean something. It's interesting that after a few months into deployments, all the males start wrestling and hugging each other on an obscene level. They grasp one another and look into each other's eyes. Then they punch and pinch until someone's legitimately hurt, just a little. I think it's a male's way to survive and thrive on deployments.

The USO tried to help by bringing cheerleaders and sexy singers to bases so they could perform for the male Soldiers, meanwhile, us females got Lt. Dan, or Gary Sinise…NOT the same thing. Though thank you Gary, you're a gentleman and a true patriot.

It's not just physical contact of the opposite sex I missed.

At that point, there was nothing I wouldn't give to be able to step outside my house and just sit in the grass and do absolutely nothing. Again, fuck pants, I couldn't wait to not wear pants for the majority of my day. I missed driving a car and going wherever the day took me. I missed cooking; chopping and sautéing things, and presenting it to Boyfriend like he was a Roman emperor.

"Come forth and eat this shit I made, you sexy beast, you," I wanted to shout to Boyfriend, but he wasn't there.

I missed baths. The showers there weren't terrible, when they worked right. One day, the base decided to try to save water, so they replaced the showerheads. The water just dribbled out and made rinsing the shampoo out of my hair a twenty-minute process. I get it, it was ridiculous for me to complain about shower pressure when there were guys out on austere bases where they had to splash water on their junk and call it clean. Misery is relative and although I know I could have had it worse, I had had it worse, so when I wanted to bitch about the shower pressure, I was going to. I ranted to my buddies until I couldn't take it anymore. During one pathetic shower, I got so pissed that I ripped the showerhead off and threw it in the trash so they'd have to replace it again, hopefully with a more powerful one. About a week later, they replaced them and the water shot out so hard, it felt like hornets attacking, it was bliss.

The other thing was, the showers were teeny tiny, so when I faced the shower curtain, my face brushed the white plastic sheet and I wondered who else's mouth had been on it. I was also aware that my ass was touching the same place as the last person's. I don't know why this bothered me. Toilet seats worked the same way and I never cared or even though twice about wiggling my ass in someone else's ass juice when I peed. I refuse to straddle toilet seats in public bathrooms. Last I checked no one has ever died from sitting on a toilet seat. Crabs maybe, but not death, and I'm too scared of the consequences of looking this up online so I'm going to go with the fact that I'm fine sitting on a public toilet seat.

I missed talking to my mom whenever I wanted.

I missed doing dishes, laundry, going to the movies, and holding hands in the dark. I missed picking out what clothes I was going to wear. I missed hugging Boyfriend before I left for work, because no one in Afghanistan cared nearly as much when I left a room as he did.

I knew how much I would appreciate all these small things that created the joy in my life at home. When I finally did get to look at Boyfriend's face and think, "hot damn, he just kissed me," I knew I would hold it so much closer. I would take the dogs on walks and rest easy knowing I didn't have to worry about a bomb hitting me, cars maybe, but not bombs.

I ached for the day I could lounge in bed and crush the dogs to death with my love. I know happiness is supposedly a state of mind, but my home, is my state of happiness. I made it back eventually, and I took a lot of baths, ate a lot of food that didn't make me shit my pants, and hugged the fur off of my boys.

# Running Somewhere

Transcendent runs in mountains and Basic Training aside, I normally prefer running on a treadmill to outside. This isn't to say I don't like running outside, but there are just too many anxieties for me to make it as enjoyable as a rubber belt headed to nowhere.

I regularly panic when crossing streets, especially at intersections where I technically have the right of way, but a car is waiting to turn. I fight the urge to throw myself on the ground and curl myself into the fetal position on the curb, so the driver absolutely knows without a doubt, I have no intention of crossing before they do. JUST GOOOO MAN.

My version of hell is getting ready to cross a street, but a car is about to turn onto where I'm supposed to cross so they slow down and I wave them to go ahead, but then they wave right back at me, because they want to shove their politeness down my throat. I start to go, but I stutter step, so they start to drive forward again, thinking I disregarded their kind gesture of letting me go, which causes me to make a sprint for it to the other side of the sidewalk. I usually do this while screaming and covering my ears. They then have the nerve to rev their engine and speed off. Well, fuck me, right?

I also assume everyone who drives by me on the street is judging how slow I'm going, "Ha, look at that Umpa Lumpa trying to go fast, how cute, ooo, ooo, look her boobs are bouncing too." This is a ridiculous thought to have because I'm on a run, working on my cardiovascular fitness so I can run up my stairs without taking a break, and those people in their cars being all unfitnessy like, driving places, so even if they did judge me, it shouldn't matter to me. It does though.

If I happen to be on a track or trail with other people way farther along the fitness scheme than I'll ever be, I feel like I compete with them, whether I want to or not. Other times, I find myself chugging along, gasping for air and I'll see someone in the distance, running in my direction. I curse at those people in my head a lot because at that precise moment, I had intended on stopping my jog and was going to begin walking. Of course, I couldn't stop then, because they'd see me slow down.

The person gets closer and I notice it's always a gorgeous woman who could be on the cover of a yoga magazine.

Seriously, why? Shouldn't they be in some Ashram doing the splits and making some other short person feel inferior? This isn't her fault though, she's gained inner beauty by drinking nothing but twig water and eating nothing but air. Those actions translate to outer beauty, and I really shouldn't hate her moisturized hair and glowing skin. She's probably the nicest person who's ever walked the earth barefoot, but I'd never know it because I'm too busy disliking her, and that's not fair.

Then I have to keep running until Aphrodite herself passes me by and she's out of sight. Yeah, she's definitely having sex tonight. I make a point to pick up corndogs on the way home.

Most importantly though, when I go on runs outside, I get lost…a lot…at any given moment in time, I have no idea where I am. I was once on a trail run with Dozer. He was super stoked about the whole thing, because of all the squirrels, and he pulled on the leash, tripping me. I was two miles into the woods and came to a fork in the trail and had no idea which route to take. I just sat on a log and cried because I couldn't figure out how to get back to the beginning. I had no cell phone and no one knew where I was. I was going to starve out there and Dozer was going to eat me because he's a selfish dick. The authorities would find my bones and the park rangers would think about renaming the trail after me in my honor, but then decide against it because no one can pronounce Bonano right. All because I was too stubborn to start yelling for help, and when I needed a dreaded stranger for once, no one else was out for a run that day.

Fuckers.

Eventually, Dozer lead me out of the trail and I sat in my car and cried some more because I desperately wanted a sense of direction, direction in anything; geography, life, goals, career, goal weight, anything. I was no closer to getting there.

That was the last trail run by myself. I've since defaulted to treadmills now. There are some drawbacks to running on them, but generally, it's a much safer bet. This doesn't mean I'm not hounded by mind noise while running. Here are some of the things I think about while on a treadmill:

I hop on a treadmill and think, whoops, this one's warped. Better delay this even more by switching to the one next to it, which is also warped, so we should try like three more to find just the right one.

Oh, look, there's even a TV in front of the treadmill I've so painstakingly picked, so I can watch the Food Network, mmm, Cupcake Wars. Then someone changes the channel to WWE wrestling and this bout is between female wrestlers in string bikinis and I hate myself even more.

It makes total sense to walk at a speed of 2mph to warm up. For all anyone knows, I'm on an incline and working astronomically hard. (psst, I'm not)

Then I get set up with my water bottle in the holder, which I'm not actually going to drink because gyms don't like it when you short out the treadmill because you couldn't get the water in your mouth while in motion.

Don't do it stranger, don't you dare get on the one next to me…they did it…QUIT LOOKING AT MY SCREEN RUNNING NEIGHBOR, ONLY GOD CAN JUDGE ME!!! In fact, Todd (males on treadmills are always named Todd), why don't you move the shit over to the one NOT next to me like I telepathically told you to do in the first place?

I really should've grabbed a towel to cover up the screen display because time is going way too slow. What if the world has ended, but I didn't hear it because I had my headphones in and I've completely missed the Rapture? So now I'm in purgatory until I've done my time. I'm not even a practicing Catholic, so I'm not sure why I think purgatory applies to me.

My boobs hurt because I just ran into the front of the fucking bar thingy on this here treadmill.

Is this going to be foooreevver…20 minutes later, still only went a mile…I want brownies.

I hope no one can hear my heavy breathing. Then I pause my music so I can hear how loud I'm breathing through my nose, as well as how loud my feet are thumping on the belt. Hippopotamus point O on the Richter scale.

Half way through the run, I start imagining a Hollywood action scene to help motivate me. To a soundtrack of Eminem, I play the hero. I must fight dozens of adversaries with a katana…and without fail I start singing to myself… "Everybody was doing martial arts fighting…da da da da da…ta ta ta." I swear, I move as fast as a teenager caught with their pants down at prom. In my head, I kick through the air and cause lots of blunt force trauma, as well as slice and dice fingers off.

I'm not sure why, but whenever I'm running, I imagine stabbing bad guys.

Meh, I'm sure it's fine. Most of the time, I'm able to sky rocket away from my inner thoughts, and it's magical. My third favorite thing in the world is when I get on a treadmill and someone else gets on the one two down from me (NOT right next to me because that's just ridiculous, again Todd, get out of my bubble Mr. Stranger Danger. I'm seriously going to flick my sweat on you after I wipe my forehead off with my hand). I create a mini race against the newcomer in my mind and when they stop and get off before I do, well, I win.

There are some days though, I can't get out of my head and it's a tad difficult to zone out. I try reenacting movie scenes in my mind, with me starring, but it doesn't always work: This reel consisted of me wielding a samurai sword and fighting Columbian drug lords, who also happen to be sex slave traffickers, because fuck those guys. If anyone deserves a good stabbing, it's them.

Then, my brain starts chiming in again:

Brain: That's all fine and dandy Laura, we fought bad guys, but why are you still running? This imaginary scenario makes no sense. Also, why are you sweating so much?

Me: Because dumbass, dudes from the cartel are still after us and we have to get away. Do you know what Los Sombreros would do if they caught us? Decapitation and penetration, that's what happens lard ass, keep running.

Brain: For starters, if they decapitated us, the penetration would be all you lady, cause I'm a brain, I go where the head goes. Also, why are you using a sword against these guys, shouldn't it be like a machete or something…ooo, do you remember the movie Machete, we should watch that again some time. Man, my thighs are touching, and these shorts are riding, people are gonna' see your celullite!!!! It hurts!!! You know, no matter how much you run, you're never going to be able to wear leather pants Laura, maybe oversized overalls, but not pants. Thirdly, don't call me a lard ass, you know that hurts my feelings, and you're better than that.

Me: Shut up you, there's more fat cells to murder! You remember Dustin don't you, he told us in 7th grade that we needed to get on a stair stepper, we need to make him pay and this is the only way. Plus, you eat too many brownies, so this running session is only leveling out our calories in vs. calories out for the binge we had yesterday.

Five minutes later:

Brain: Are we done yet, faaack this is stupid, we're not even going anywhere. Seriously, I wanna' put a brownie in my mouth, so how about you get off this dumb thing and we can run to a brownie shop instead? I mean, we already did this like a day ago and now everything hurts. This is straight abuse, and it's so hard to keep my arms going. You really don't need to fit into your pants, you can totally just buy a bigger size. Hell, screw pants, we don't need them, we never have, why do you insist on pants Laura…why do you hate me so much?

Me: No, we agreed, we'd go five miles today and I'm not giving you brownies, you addict, you. What if there's an accident one day and you have to run for help, but because

YOU didn't want to run, we're too slow getting help and before you know it, that hitchhiker we picked up is going to bleed out and die? Do you really want Harold's death on your conscience, huh, do you?

Brain: Who the shit is Harold?????!!!

Me: Oh look, it's been fifty minutes, we can stop now.

Brain: You're an asshole...can I please have a brownie now?

Me: Probably. Yes.

# I Know What Skinny Feels Like and It Doesn't Fit

As the majority of females on this planet, I have obviously swam through the feces infested pit of dieting and health experts (as well as people flapping their gums with no real expertise) telling me what I should and shouldn't do to get healthy. Alright, we all know what they mean when they say healthy, they mean skinny. I bought into it for so long.

They said eat this, don't touch that, pop this pill, run those miles, or cinch this wrap thingy around your stomach overnight while it's also slopped down with shrinking cream.

I was advised to start juicing to cleanse my bunghole shoot and I should also get fiber. But I threw away the pulp, so I'm not sure where that fiber is going to come from. I could've gone Paleo, where critics of the diet swore I'd have a heart attack before I could inhale the five pounds of bacon I just made.

Also, there's the Zone. With this diet, I had to figure in different calculations like my weight, age and activity level…there's math involved, I dunno', I gave it the old Community College try. Foods are assigned "block" numbers and I was told I should have a certain amount of blocks throughout the day, breaking down how many grams of protein, carbs, and fats I should eat. That lasted about a week until I poured sugar from a box directly into my mouth, chased with beer. Hey, it was raw sugar so it's fine.

I could have eaten meat on Atkins, but then I couldn't snort bleached flour up my nose, so that was a no-go.

A big thing was, everyone said I had to absolutely eat clean. This meant no processed foods and no artificial ingredients. THEY also said I had to actually clean my fruit with special wax dissolving solvents, but I should try to keep THE fruits sort of dirty so the dirt would do something, something in my belly, PROBIOTICS!

Television said I could try toning up with a Shake Weight. Over and over people screamed at me to guzzle more fats, but only if it's a good one, like the old disgustingly textured avocado…fuck you Subway, avocados are gross. I could add lemon juice, salt and pepper, or bake an egg in one or spread that green goop on my toast all day long. I'm still going to dry heave when I try to swallow avocados. The only reference to avocados I've ever enjoyed was watching Cannibal Women in the Avocado Jungle of Death, featured on USA UP All Night!

Books tell me I better damn well drop that potato because…CARBS!!!

Well, there are good carbs too, like sweet potatoes. I have one thing to say to sweet potatoes. You are a faker. It's not really helpful when you only taste delicious when I put brown sugar on you….mmmm, brown sugar.

I was told I had to be sure I got more macros, or was it micros? I don't fuckin' know, I'm not a scientist. I could count my points with Jenny. Question, has anyone ever seen Jenny Craig…I mean, I have no idea what she looks like. I picture her sitting at a computer watching cat videos, dipping Doritos in chocolate, but is somehow still thin. I picture her getting printouts of everyone's weight in the nation and maniacally laughing. I'm not even going to look her picture up. I want to live with the mystery.

Experts shout, "Eat every three hours," because yeah, I have a fridge in my car. They also suggested maybe trying to fast in the mornings and to drink some lemon juice with cayenne pepper, or drink Slim Fast because everyone loves almost gritty and not quite chocolate tasting liquid paste.

I know it's important to eat fruit, but wait, maybe I shouldn't because there's too much sugar. Well, ok, I could have like one fruit, but it better be the tart shit I don't like, like grapefruit. I'd like to poke people in the eye who tell me to eat grapefruit because then their eye will feel as bad as my mouth.

People swear those sour fruits will taste sweet eventually, if, and only if, I don't eat a granule of sugar elsewhere. If I must have sweetness, I was told, try maple syrup, rice syrup, honey, Truvia, Stevia, Sweet and Low, Splenda. Then, I read artificial sweeteners probably cause cancer. Oh just fucking splendid, but so does air, so whatever.

Obviously, I agreed that I should eat more vegetables, but apparently, they better not have any pesticides on them or I'll grow more legs. I think. Also, CANCER again…that's what I've heard anyways. Organic veggies are the best, but you better start eating them in the car on the way home from the grocery store, or they'll go bad.

Green beans, corn, tomatoes, you know the good tasting "veggies", aren't even vegetables. Reportedly, legumes can be inflammatory. Inflaming my ass sphincter is right…something, something, also nightshade "vegetables" can be bad for you. Yum, chard and kale are way better anyways.

I've heard conflicting things about white rice. Some say it is good for your stomach and a good carb, but in reality I should eat brown rice instead because WHOLE GRAINS, wait no, WHOLE WHEAT, wait what??? What the actual fuck is the difference between whole grain and whole wheat…isn't wheat a grain. I don't know, I'm not a farmer.

Either way, GLUTEN!!!…everyone slaps bread out of my hands.

I should definitely get more protein, but again, not from beans because they inflame your….stuff. I suppose I could get it from yogurt, but I've been told it sure as hell better only be plain Greek yogurt, which, come on people, is basically sour cream, IT'S SOUR CREAM. But wait, I could totally put some of those tart ass blueberries in it to sweeten up my sour cream. Or, I could put my yogurt on sweet potatoes and pretend it is in fact sour cream, win-win situation.

I've been menacingly warned I shouldn't get protein from yogurt, because yeah, it's dairy. And dairy, in theory, makes everyone's hormones weird and our sinuses flemmy. Milk does build stronger bones from the calcium, but spinach has more calcium than milk. So, I should go ahead and eat five pounds of spinach per sitting for my bones.

Don't forget, milk is "animal puss", as I've heard it called. I've heard if I'm going to drink milk, it should be skim milk because fat free is the way to go. Wait, what did you say, Mr. Health Guru out there in the interwebs? I should drink full fat milk and not low-fat milk? Well, which the shit is it, whole or skim? I will put a squirt gun of milk to my head until you tell me for sure which one I should drink.

Well, I think I would be better off drinking rice, soy, coconut, or almond milk. Meh, not so much soy, soy's not good for you, something about soilent…I don't remember.

I know I should run and lift weights, but maybe not, it might be bad for my knees and joints…or it could be, maybe, not sure. I suppose I could get hit by a car running, so probably, I should just trip around on a treadmill instead, staring at the wall.

Zumba (dancing in a group exercise class), can be fun, but only for people that have the same DNA makeup of Shakira or J-LO.

As a woman, I've been told I shouldn't lift weights too much, or I'll get bulky. Fuck you Pat, the lady who didn't think I could carry a 20lb box out to my car once. I can deadlift 200 plus pounds. Also, I haven't worked my biceps out in over a year and I'm already bulky so I don't think it can get much worse. I'm also aware that I shouldn't be too skinny either, because strangers will tell me to eat a sandwich and that I'm not a real woman because I don't have curves. You know what makes me a real woman? Because I say so, and I don't have a plastic mound over my genitals so I'm going to go ahead and call myself a real woman. That's what makes me a real woman.

It's been reported that body builders have bad mobility at times, runners can be too scrawny, Crossfitters just assholes (that's the public's consensus, not mine). Yogi's are too granola-ee and smell funny.

I can't stress this enough, I must drink gallons of water, while trying to keep my day job. Unfortunately, my job doesn't include spending the day writing reports up in the bathroom, so I gotta' piss on my own time.

Let's talk about chocolate. It can actually be good for me, but only if it's so and so percent Cocoa, cocoah, cacao..cocaine…whatever, shakes fist…so basically, you're eating chalk.

Go for it though, antioxidants!

Where there's chocolate, there's peanut butter. Now, peanut butter is a good source of fat and protein, but factories add a whole lot of sugar in each jar. Therefore, I should only eat all-natural peanut butter. Better yet, I could do all-natural almond butter and I can even make it at home yay!!! I've had almond butter. It's like taking an almond flavored caulking tube and squirting it in your mouth. MMM, put that on some motherloving toast and you've got yourself a breakfast of champs…I mean mediocres, because then you'd be eating bread. Another hand comes out of the void and slaps the bread out of my hands.

Salmon, I have nothing nice to say about salmon so I won't say anything at all. Ok, I'll say a little something, OMEGAS something or other, FATTY, and ACIDS.

Salmon is reportedly good for me but again, it's an animal so maybe I shouldn't fuck the planet up more by eating it and if I do eat it, I should have a side of guilt with it.

But mostly, COCONUT!!!!

As in coconut milk, butter, oil, meal, flour, sweetener, water, toothpaste and lotion. I should just totally immerse my entire body in a tub of coconut oil, then I'll open my mouth, and swish it all around. That, my dear friends, is called oil pulling, the mouth swishy thing with coconut oil. It apparently pulls bacteria out of your mouth, and can whiten teeth. I mean, myself, I'm not sucking on bandages, so I think I'm good. I don't absolutely have to oil pull. I've been told I should eat coconut flesh, wash it all down with coconut water, and just bask in the feeling of the floaty flakes at the bottom of the can that found their way into my throat. Then, I'll use that water to take some probiotics for my digestive tract. Supposedly because we wash our food off, it doesn't have dirt on it and we don't get enough probiotics...SCIENCE!

This advice is just the tip of the banana; the different things I've heard throughout my life about losing weight and being healthy.

You know what I said?

I quit.

I knew all along what it took to be slender and healthy. I knew what it took to simply lose weight, and I wasn't going to follow the prescription anymore; the prescription of forcing things down my throat that I couldn't stand. What's the point in being skinny if I wanted to die and I was grumpy all the time? Forever after, I was going to do what felt good. Fortunately, smoothies packed full of nasty spinach can be punched up in deliciousness with some apples and actual sweet tasting fruit. That, my friends, feels good.

# One Dose Away From Fine

One sunny and quiet afternoon I answered the phone and heard my roommate over the line. Her voice was shaky, but she got to the point quickly. I wasn't as shocked as I could have been, given I'd gotten this type of call before.

"I can't believe he did it, it's so selfish," she said amongst the details.

I clamped my mouth shut. I wanted to scream at her, but I didn't, she was in pain and that was her way of dealing with her anger. She told me of the suicide of a soldier we had deployed with the previous year. I stayed silent and let her speak the thousand thoughts that always run through someone's mind when they've found out someone they know killed themselves. I couldn't be mad at her for what she said because it was how she felt.

The general public has a lot of opinions and thoughts on suicide, some of them never going through suicidal thoughts themselves. "There were no signs," they often say. "They weren't experiencing anything that bad really. They seemed fine. They're cowards, how could they do that to their loved ones? Their life seemed on track. I didn't see it coming. How could they? Were their problems that awful? Why didn't anyone notice? Why didn't they reach out, or speak up, tell someone?"

I felt in my saturated ventricles that those who took their own lives weren't cowards. They were just alone.

It's easy for 'normal' people to point fingers and imply depression is all in the head. The phrase of, "Stop being sad," is supposed to kick us out of our despair. I have been told that things will get better so I just must hang on. I have been told I just need to stick it out. Too many times I've heard these people using the word coward for those who said enough.

No one knows what monsters the deceased already triumphed over, before they took their own lives. No one knows the strength of the missed ones. No one knows how the broken ones gathered their last ounce of defiance to make it as far as they did, and that was the victory, that they hadn't gone sooner.

The same people, who cursed those for leaving too soon, didn't know about the many faces of doubt and stifling hopelessness already faced. Suicidal people were not selfish. They were hurting. They were facing the unbeatable despair of living in a world they felt would never stop bludgeoning them. It was too much. They made one last stand to outrun the demons, and sometimes they didn't make it.

No, I don't believe those who commit suicide gave up, they just took a different route around their pain. The only route they felt could offer them relief. I'm not advocating or canonizing suicide here. Make no mistake, ending anyone's' life is a big deal, including ending your own. I am simply refusing to speak ill of those who made that choice.

I always felt no one could understand what suicidal ideation felt like unless they'd been there. In my head, the people who insisted that the battered and dented legion stay in this world were selfish. The non-damaged were asking sad souls to stay and endure the pain, just so the 'normals' wouldn't feel sad when the others were gone.

Even though I had these thoughts too, I wasn't ready to go.

I started counseling after my first deployment to Iraq in 2008. It's something I still depend on today. I never bought into the stigma of seeking help when I needed it. Our culture tells us Soldiers fight against therapy. Service members reportedly feel like it shows them as weak if they try to talk about their problems. Granted, I hadn't gone through what a lot of other Soldiers went through, but that doesn't mean I didn't have my pain too, in and out of the military. I had seen the worst of what people were capable of and my mind couldn't smooth it over

Couple this with the trauma of being in an abusive relationship, and life overall, I had been through the 'heavy soiled' cycle of life and things weren't getting any better. I hadn't worked for over a year, and I no longer looked forward to the next day, or the next hour. I felt useless and every minute became excruciating. I arrived at the point I felt ready to say I needed to talk some things out.

I walked into the VA and asked to see a therapist. The receptionist checked her computer and said there wasn't anyone available to see me for a month from then. I guess she saw my face crumple in panic.

"Do you think you can wait until then?" she asked.

I shook my head no and my eyes welled up with tears. Ok, we've already established I cry a lot, so let's ignore it happened again.

Ten minutes later, I was sitting in a chair across from a social worker and I walked out of the building knowing I could make it to the next day. I could make it to my appointment with my assigned counselor. That was all I needed to stay alive.

I started the sessions and mostly my counselor nodded her head and occasionally said things that made me feel better. We talked about my past, but more often than not, we talked about Boyfriend. He never knew this though. After all, we were only dating at the time and didn't live together yet. We lived about 90 miles away from each other. This pretty much gave him the go ahead to decide that what happened in Muncie, where he lived, stayed in Muncie. The only problem for him was, I'd find out about his indiscretions occasionally. I would tell my therapist, she would tell me I didn't deserve to have the person I loved cheat on me, I'd ignore her advice, and I would continue loving Boyfriend anyways. As you can see, this made it hard to have an optimistic outlook on life. Someone once told me that it was my fault. They said people only do to us what we allow them to, and I guess, she wasn't wrong.

Over the years, as I stayed with Boyfriend and went on another couple deployments, I went through two more therapists. Every time I returned home from another tour, I checked in with the VA and was assigned a new doctor. It wasn't that the deployments made me depressed, it was more coming back to a life I didn't know what to do with that made me depressed.

The therapist I'm seeing now is probably my favorite. She's smaller than me, her voice is like my grandma's, and her eyes are always kind.

Fast track to 2017, and I had been seeing her for a few weeks but things weren't getting any better. I initially started the sessions because even though it was two years later, I wasn't dealing well with the breakup with Boyfriend and I felt stuck. The stagnation turned to sadness, the sadness turned to despair, and the despair turned to numbness and for Christ's sake, feeling nothing was worse than feeling pain. I filled out surveys the Army sent me, and one after another alerted me to the fact that I was merely surviving life. Did I maybe need to talk to someone, the online questionnaires always questioned with the questions.

"I fucking AM talking to someone!" I would scream at my computer screen. "I still want to fall asleep and not wake up for fuck's sake." I was walking around and breathing, moving through the days, but I wasn't seeking, hearing, or diving into the meat of it all.

My therapist asked me one day what I wanted from our time together. I put my fist over my chest and looked at her.

"I want to rip out the last shred of wanting someone to care about. I want to stop the desire of needing anyone. I don't want it anymore. Can you help me do that?" I asked. She looked at me, very sad in that moment.

For the longest time, I thought my depression was situational. I thought, "Hey, some really shitty things have happened to me, and once all the shitty stuff stops, I'll be alright, I've made it through every other time, so it'll all be fine eventually."

The real problem was, even when the shitty stuff stopped, I still felt hollow and at the same time as if some tragedy had befallen me but I didn't know what that thing was. Like some awful dream when I wake up to and feel sucked dry of any pleasure I've ever had in my life, but then I always realize it was just a dream so I start to warm up to the idea that I can look forward to life. Only, during that time, my dread never left. I always felt like something was wrong, even when I couldn't point my finger at the situation and scream, "It's YOU, you're the problem."

It was like the Great Nothingness that Atreyu fought in *The Neverending Story*, and that nothingness in my life literally felt like it was never going to end and I also had a horse that was going to drown in mud forever, and that was how life was going to be now, and forever.

I'd been splurging my guts to my therapist for weeks and I railed against the idea of medication until I realized things weren't getting better on their own, and frankly, the shitty stuff was never going to go away anyways, so I'd have to figure out a way to deal with it always being there in some way. I didn't want to walk around in the same clothes for days anymore. I didn't want to lie on the kitchen floor staring at the ceiling anymore, I wanted to brush my teeth again. Hell, I wanted to enjoy eating pizza again at least.

I told my therapist I was ready to give medication a try and we decided I should try taking an antidepressant. I had the mediocre hope it would bring back some semblance of joy. I then met with a psychiatrist and she put me on medication.

I was in my second or so week of taking the meds when I had my monthly Army obligation in Indiana. Now, I feel like the general population thinks that all Soldiers do is learn to kill things and shoot a lot of guns. Contrary to this belief, most Reserve Soldiers (Weekend Warriors) only go to a gun range about twice a year. This is when we attempt to qualify as being proficient in shooting firearms.

This weekend, I was riding in a van out to a firing range in order to qualify with a pistol. The goal was to hit so many targets out of so many targets and prove I could save my country from terrorists if need be. I sat in the back seat and had an idea hit me like a brick, so I started to have a string of peculiar thoughts in the form of an argument with myself:

Brain: What if I squirreled away a 9mm round (bullet) into my pocket?

Me: Why would you do that Laura?

Brain: Well, we'd put it in our pocket, then go into a bathroom with our assigned Beretta, nothing more than that, I swear.

Me: Ok, just say we take it into a bathroom, that's all we have to do? Just hide it, take it into one of those plastic Porta Potties, and hang out for a bit? I don't know if I feel comfortable with that. What else could we do?

Brain: I don't know, we don't have to do anything particular. Let's just see what happens. We don't even have to put it in a pocket, if we put it there, it's like we're meaning to hide it. We can put it in one of those pouches on our Army vest that we usually put candy in. I mean, a round could easily fall into that pocket, it's basically the same thing as accidently bringing it into the bathroom with us. It wouldn't be too crazy to load the gun with a single little round. Just one round.

Me: But, that doesn't make sense. Things are fine, you shouldn't be so dramatic. Pull your shit together, take the next step and handle what the fuck the world has in mind for us today. We're going to go shoot at targets and we're going to call it a day. I know what you're doing here brain. I know you're trying to end things, but things aren't that bad.

Brain: Look, things aren't that bad, but they're not that good either. What's the point? The best things that have ever happened are over and done with. Chances are, you've already felt as happy as you're ever going to feel and was that really all that great? We're made up of atoms that used to be stardust, and those atoms don't even touch each other.

They're just in a shitty configuration you call that lumpy body of yours, and those atoms are floating, full of space, and that doesn't even amount to a speck of meaning anything in this fucking ginormous galaxy. Even if we bought into the idea that there's something to keep suffering for, it'll only break our entire body into even more shards of broken shit, right at the moment we think it's ok to be happy. These people here with us, in this place we stumble around with are shit. You think they love you and care about you. Well, you thought that about a lot of people and look where it got us. You try to keep caring about things, but you know what Laura, I'm fucking tired. Do you hear me? I'm tired. I can't let another person hurt us like that, and you know that is the only reason they exist, to hurt us. Also, we're always going to be fat because you're lazy, and as much as you don't want to admit it, that bothers you even though you think it's shallow. You're going to be alone, at the end of all of this, it's just you, no matter what. So really, let's call it a day because obviously happiness just isn't in the cards for us. Look, just slip the round into a pouch, go to the bathroom, load the round, put the barrel against that spot on your temple, the part you rub when you have a headache. We don't have to do anything after that. But if we did, if we pulled, imagine how nice it would be. So quiet. Not another fucking person would touch us again. We could rest. We could leave this shit show.

Me: I feel like this is a trick. You're a liar.

I sat in the van, staring into space as the shouting took place inside my head. No one else in the van spoke.

This wasn't a new phenomenon, the suicidal thoughts. But usually, as soon as I'd start thinking about drunkenly getting into my running car parked in a garage, but before I could formulate the actual plan, my emotions usually kicked in and tackled the destructive thoughts, purely because they wanted to survive. In the past, my emotions wanted to inhale everything that ever was, ever is, and ever would be. Over the years, my survival instincts always kicked in and the suicidal thoughts were driven out before I could even form an actual plan.

This time was different. My emotions were tired. Everything hurt, my heart, my lungs, my joints, everything.

That day, the scenario played out in my head to the very end of what would happen if I pulled the trigger.

I rationally knew these thoughts shouldn't be happening. I contemplated turning to the person next to me in the van and telling them what the shadows were whispering into my ears. I waited for myself to spring into action against the thoughts. That's the thing with my depression. It leached any fight I had left. I thought about putting the gun to my head and pulling the trigger, just as I usually thought about buying toilet paper, it just needed to be done. I wasn't sad, I wasn't scared, I was just annoyed with my argumentative mind and all I really wanted was to be left in peace. I wanted the people that cared about me to not exist, so I wouldn't feel guilty about leaving. It had been such a long war and I was ready to surrender. Fuck everyone else, I thought. They would all move on with life after I was gone and their lives wouldn't change.

Many times, when I heard about a famous person committing suicide, my first thought was that of jealousy. I know, I know, it's disgusting to think that way and how dare I, but that's what I felt, I could never hide from it. I was jealous because they'd been able to do something I couldn't do.

Fortunately, among the bottom layer of all the thoughts I had, was one last cry that I couldn't ignore.

Wait, no, fuck no, we're not doing this. We've been here before, not today Satan, not today. What if it's just the medication talking? Sometimes that happens to people, the pills make things worse. At the very least, let's give it a week, maybe change prescriptions and if things still suck, we can come up with something else.

I don't know where the rationality came from. It was enough to convince me things were going to be ok.

Until three days later.

I had decided to get weekday drunk and I sat in my living room sucking down beer and watching bad movies. I began the thought process of asking myself questions. Just exactly how many milligrams of my sleeping medication would be enough to do it?

Six hundred milligrams, that's how much I'd need to go to sleep forever. I walked upstairs to my bedroom, sat on my bed, counted out how many pills would equal 600 milligrams and I stared at the tiny white chalky pills.

Because the alcohol was shutting out some of the picture, I don't remember a lot of what happened after that. I don't remember what battle raged that night. I do know I put them back into the bottle and I tried to go to sleep. At some point, I grabbed them again, poured some out into my hand and popped them into my mouth. Luckily, it wasn't the lethal dose.

The next morning, I woke up hung over and still so tired. My body ached and my stomach quivered. I made it out of the trenches though and immediately decided I would tell my therapist what had happened.

At my next appointment, I slurred out all the details of wanting to end my life. My doctor went into crisis mode, immediately called the psychiatrist that prescribes me my medicine and I met with her to talk about switching them out. I then went back to my usual therapist and we made a safety plan, writing down everything, because who doesn't like a to-do list for those "crazy" moments? We wrote down the warning signs of another episode, coping strategies. It listed whom I would call if I had the thoughts again, and finally how to make my environment safe in case I couldn't make it through the other steps.

Now, whenever I need a sleeping pill, my mother has to give it to me and she hides the bottle so I can't find it. Again, a lesson I wouldn't forget, I will always need my mom.

After taking my new medication, the thoughts are mostly nonexistent. They're not completely gone, but more like something in my peripheral vision, just sneaking past the point where I turn my head to see them face on. I'm ok with this, as it still allows me to meet each new day, shitty or not. To me, that's a win. I know what the darkness feels like, and I'm ready for the next time. Now, I have all the candles, flashlights, and lamps in my arsenal to fight it, and I have backup.

# I Don't Know How Serial Killers Do It

My phone buzzed one day and it was a text from my grandpa, bless his heart, who manages to stay with the times at 81-years-old. He asked if I wanted to go turtle fishing with him. I mean, in theory, it should be called turtle hunting, not fishing, which sounds a lot cooler, because fishing implies catching fish, hence the word fish. Catching turtles should obviously be called turtle hunting, or wait, maybe turtling.

It wasn't a strange request for me, I'd been hunting with him before and we had a mutual respect thing going on. He was a hard working man who had tried his best in life and was verifiably a badass, what with his cowboy boots and cowboy hat, but also tender in that grandpa kind of loving way. I love my grandpa and spending time with him was important to me no matter what we were doing, so I said yes, even though I wasn't extremely excited. He sent back a message giving the details, followed by a string of cowboy hat emoji's because, well, he's a cowboy.

The next day, we drove an hour to the lake and set the boat upon the shore. As we pushed out into the water, the boat started to tip and sway as grandpa crawled to his seat. Look, he's aged superbly well over the years and still remains active. This doesn't change the fact that I thought he was going to tip the boat over because I don't care if an Olympic gymnast was in it, that tin can of a boat was a rockin', and it would have been hard for anyone to keep their balance. I rehearsed in my head just exactly how I would save grandpa from the four-inch deep water. I came to the conclusion we'd both just have to die. When it comes to me being around water, I'm reduced to an incompetent five-year-old and I'm very uncomfortable with my odds of surviving a drowning scenario.

I'm assuming most people don't exactly know how turtle fishing works, so I'll give a rundown. Get yourself some old meat that you maybe just couldn't make time to cook that week, stick it on some hooks (special hooks that I don't know the name of). Then you tie those hooks to some sturdy lines (strings) and tie those strings to wooden blocks. The goal was to wrap those blocks around tree limbs and floating vegetation along the banks.

It was quiet except for that whole nature sound that makes you feel all Jane Goodally. I enjoyed the warmth on my skin and the twerting of birds in my ears, as we skimmed the sparkling water in our little dinghy. Of course I'm not super comfortable with silence, so I had to fill it with dumb words.

"Ya' hear the latest on Trump, grandpa?" I asked. Not a day went by that our POTUS wasn't in the news. I wasn't sure what else to talk about as me and grandpa didn't exactly share the same interests, besides karaoke, he loves karaoke.

"Oh that guy, I'm so sick of hearing about that guy," grandpa grumbled. "I'm sick of looking at his face too. You know what that guy looks like?"

"What does he look like?" I asked with a smile.

"He looks like a cocksucker is what he looks like," he advised. "He's all..." Then grandpa formed his mouth into the familiar round shape of an O and shook his head back and forth, simulating the sucking of the D. I sputtered a giggle and closed my eyes, trying to black out the vision of what I'd just witnessed.

The tricky part about turtle fishing is finding a place to tie the strings. I'm not super familiar with what makes an ideal snapping turtle hangout. To this day, I wonder if they float around aimlessly; are they always on the lookout for food, do they sleep with their heads tucked into their shells, do they congregate together, snapping at each other? I don't know, I have so many questions. But apparently they prefer to be along the banks of the river, among lily pads and downed trees.

I do not enjoy venturing into places these delicious turtles live. I have to say though, I was pretty impressed with myself as I only had about three jerky-fear-seizures caused by spider webs. A few times my head nudged into a thick ass web along the route. I started my murder spree by stomping no less than five creepy crawlers in the boat. Grandpa decided it was my time to become an adult at 32-years-old and he let me handle them myself. "Go out and conquer," he said. I couldn't go no fucking where, I was in a boat, but I handled business and came out a warrior.

We eventually tied all the lines we had, and because the actual catching of the turtle takes some time, we headed back to shore for lunch.

It was late afternoon time, so the bar we walked into was almost empty. Grandpa said he remembered they had good food at the dive bar. Once we stepped inside, the musty room felt like we were trespassing. It was as if we were seeing something during the day that usually only came out at night. I didn't have a habit of going into bars during daylight hours. We sat down and ordered food.

There's always that one regular bar customer that sways, smokes, and cackles louder than sober people do. He walked in, tottering on his feet already, asking for a Bloody Mary, followed by another request for more vodka. We tried to ignore the crude way in which the guy was trying to hit on the waitress.

Grandpa whispered to the waitress, "That jackass doesn't respect women at all, how can you stand dealing with that crap?"

"Gotta' make tips hun," she replied as she served our burgers.

Once we returned to the lake, my stomach filled with anticipation of getting bites on the lines. The sun crashed through the branches along the banks and dove into the deeper water, creating light slices that revealed empty hooks. The first few lines were duds, but we soon saw one was taut, leading into the murky water.

"I see bubbles," I said a little too loudly given the gravity of the situation. I pulled the line up, and sure as boys won't call you back after the first date sure, there was a ten-pound turtle on the hook. Obviously grandpa pulled it in because I'm not familiar at all with the stretching and biting capabilities of snapping turtles so I wasn't going to wrangle one into the boat. I've seen them use their jaws to crush through apples and, frankly, I like having all my fingers, for fingering, er I mean handling things.

"You just gotta' stay away from that end," grandpa said pointing to the head.

To my slight discomfort, we put the small turtle into a heavy-duty burlap sack. The snapper hissed and moved around inside. I worried it was scared and I cursed myself for having a conscience when I knew full well what was going to go down later.

We ended up pulling two more 25-pounders into the boat. Satisfied with our survival expedition for the day, we headed home. Grandpa would butcher them in his garage at home. I had the added benefit of living right next door to him. I also must preface this by saying there is a brewery establishment nestled in our back alley. The back patio, where hipsters and jivers dine and drink full-bodied beers (whatever that means), faced the opening of the garage.

We had a few looks from the patrons, as we pulled the bag out of the tailgate of the truck. The turtles wrestled around within the bag. I assume it looked like a grown ass adult had been kidnapped, but we soon proved we weren't human murderers by letting the turtles out of the sack. All the eyes of the customers widened as we dumped the turtles out onto the ground. It's easy eating meat when people don't have to watch the cycle of life right before their eyes as they enjoy said meat.

We set up the work station; getting knives, a hose to wash the blood out of the garage, paper towels and grandpa's trusty two-by-four. To be as humane as possible, he whacks the turtles in the face with the wood to knock them out, you know, before the cutting of the head off. This was always a hard part for me to watch, as generally, I apologize to ants when I accidently step on them. Not spiders though, they have it coming. In fact, I believe there is a network of spiders that consistently only attack me while I'm sitting on the toilet, when I'm at my most vulnerable. They must have given word to the lake spiders to let them know I was coming.

Grandpa knocked the first small turtle out and began cutting its head off with a box cutter. Unfortunately, the skin was too tough so he couldn't get through it with the blade. He then grabbed a hatchet and started chopping at the half-decapitated head. I was bent down, holding onto the tail as he hacked away, blood splattering inside my ear canal and onto my face.

"I don't like this anymore," I cried. My sobs coincided with each blow of the hatchet and I was sure I was the evilest person on the planet. How old was this turtle to have lived long enough to grow this big, did it have babies that would miss it, or a mother that woke up, never to see her son again. Shit.Got.Deep.

"It's not dead yet, it's still moving, oh my God this is awful!" I sobbed at that point, still maintaining control of the tail through my sniffling. Some of the drinkers on the patio changed seats to a further spot away from the gruesome scene.

"It's alright Laura, it's dead, it's just the nerves and muscles having spasms," he reassured me.

I watched him butcher the rest of the meat, watching every knife slice so that I could do it on the next turtle. I told myself that it was ok to kill the turtles. My family was on hard times and we needed the food. After all, I wasn't working. I also reminded myself that the apocalypse was coming one day and this chubby girl is going to eat by golly because I'm a motherfucking Maggie and not a Lori.

Grandpa finished carving all the meat from the shell and we moved onto the next one, so much larger than the last. He pummeled it with the wood and I told him I would do the rest of it. I started cutting the head off but once again the knife wasn't sharp enough so the skin wouldn't cut. I then grabbed the hatchet and finished the job, saying sorry the entire time. I looked down and there was blood spattered on my bare legs, and all I could do was scream/cry, "HOW THE FUCK DO SERIAL KILLERS DO THIS?"

# Why is There a Toothbrush on a Stairway in Afghanistan

I was on an unnumbered week in Afghanistan, walking to the chow hall for breakfast. I had been overseas for a few months. The same repeated day over and over. Wake up, brush teeth, get dressed, go to work, play monopoly, (because really...that's all the regular Army does on deployments – not true...or is it), break for lunch, go back to work, go to the gym, waste the last hour of the day ordering things online, then go back to room, and go to sleep.

That day, there would probably be turkey, peas, absolutely a salad, and ice cream. This was a safe part of Afghanistan after all, where ice cream could survive the heat. I walked my usual route to lunch, dragging my feet on the dusty road. Then I saw it.

Lying in the dirt was a blue and white toothbrush. I stopped and looked at the sad and wilted bristles. I kicked it with my tan boot. There were no bathrooms nearby. Come on universe, I complained, I hadn't figured the last one out, why was this toothbrush in my path? My brain stopped working. It didn't want to think up a story as to how it got there. I wished I'd had my camera, I thought. I wanted to take a picture of it. But then, what the fuck would I do with a picture of a toothbrush spotted in Afghanistan? I guess I wanted a picture to prove to other people the absolute saturated phenomenon of toothbrushes out in the wild. I mean, I'm assuming most people don't grasp their presence, but they're out there.

Another few months later, I took a helicopter and a flight towards home, back to Indiana. I had severed ties with Boyfriend by that time, I had quit my civilian job, and didn't know what I'd be returning to. My unit was waiting in a dark plastic tent on the next part of the trip.

I sat on the metal chair that was made specifically NOT to sleep on because sleep is for the weak. I remembered how I got there, at that exact moment, that tent in a foreign country. I went over it all. I was 31-years-old, single and unemployed. It wasn't too difficult to follow the trail of my past to my current situation.

In high school, I followed a boy and that boy lead me to social work and the degree I would eventually earn. That boy left. Then, I had loved a boy named Jon, but he died while I was in college. Because I didn't know how to deal with his death, I vowed to honor what he loved, so I joined the Army after college. While in the Army, I met Boyfriend. I was never meant to grow old with Boyfriend, but he introduced me to the person that would send me to a school through the Army to become a journalist. I would learn to write again, from scratch, planting the seed of what I was to become. Years later, Marie would convince me to deploy with her unit, where I would have enough pain and time to write a book. The time away from Boyfriend would show me that he wasn't THE ONE, he was just ONE, amongst the many. If I hadn't broken up with Boyfriend, I never would have moved to Missouri, where I learned to be alone. If I hadn't fallen out of favor with Marie, I never would have moved back home to Indiana, and I wouldn't have returned to my old Army unit where I met the editor of this here book you're reading. Without that editor, I would have had a shitty manuscript, where no one could get past the typos, and I would have sunk into obscurity, stay tuned for that one. My editor is now one of my very closest friends, making the rough days bearable by getting me to try root beer floats for the very first time. Without this book, I would have had no reason to get out of bed once I returned home from the last deployment.

So, I'm not saying that everything happens for a reason. I'm saying that in everything that happens, I've found my reasons.

I think back to the trip home from Afghanistan. I had served my time and my unit began the trip home, which would take roughly four days. We landed at an airfield and were told we had about seventeen hours until the next leg of the trip. I made several trips to the bathroom to try to pass the time, smoked a lot of cigarettes, tried sleeping upright in an uncomfortable chair, and played cards with some friends. As night turned into day, Marie said she was hungry. We both agreed to go get food, so we left the stifling tent, along with a few other Soldiers. I walked with Marie up a staircase built into a sand hill. It led to the tents where we could find all the sandwiches our hearts desired. We grabbed what food and drink we could, and then made the walk back to where we would await our flight back to the states. We were all tired, as we hadn't seen an actual bed in over two days. As I put one foot down in front of the other, I fixed my gaze on the stairs. They were manmade and awkward to navigate. Because I was tired, I willed my legs to work as I trekked down the terrain. It was the early morning hours and no one else was around. The chill in the air breezed around me as I watched my breath seep out of my mouth. I looked down while walking and saw it, another toothbrush, this time it was purple.

Three's a charm right?

Made in the USA
Columbia, SC
03 March 2018